autism
&alleluias

Advance Praise for
Autism & Alleluias

"I was deeply moved by Kathleen Deyer Bolduc's book about her journey with her son Joel. Most autism resources are either clinical in nature or deceptively upbeat and sugary sweet. While Kathy acknowledges 'slogging through the wet cement' of her days, her extraordinary book is about valuing, honoring, and enjoying the unexpected gifts of her son." —Ginny Thornburgh, program director, Interfaith Initiative, American Association of People with Disabilities, Washington, DC

"Story by story, Kathy Bolduc leads us through the plunging despair and soaring joy that will resonate with others who have the awesome responsibility of raising a child with significant developmental challenges. Her stories, interspersed with prayers and poems, are instructive at a deep level. She does not presume to provide recipes for conquering the constant challenges of daily life. Instead, she provides us with her deeply personal journal as a mother of a son with autism. We learn with her that by drawing on the deep wellsprings of faith, laments transform to alleluias." —Diana Garland, PhD, dean, Baylor School of Social Work, Waco, Texas

"Kathy Bolduc masterfully weaves together her stories of living life with her son Joel while holding the hand of her Lord and Savior Jesus Christ. The challenges, joys, and learning that have filled her life because of Joel's presence are artfully presented in a way that will inform and encourage the reader. I see this book not only as a valuable resource for family members living with autism, but a necessary part of our church libraries as we all learn to better understand and include our brothers and sisters in Christ." —Barbara J. Newman, CLC Network church consultant and author of *Autism and Your Church*

"Grounded by her faith, Kathy Bolduc engages important matters all too often avoided—from accepting Joel's distinctly un-Presbyterian worship style to appreciating his sexual identity as a young man. It's a candid book about a Christian response to those devalued by the larger world. Belonging is rooted in listening and understanding; it's not about 'fixing' or finding a missing piece of the puzzle." —Milton Tyree, consultant, Presbyterians for Disability Concerns

"Kathy is a guiding light to us in how to walk through this world with faith that God's peace and blessings do endure despite life's struggles and challenges. Parents and caregivers will find a spiritual connection and divine treasures in reading *Autism & Alleluias*." —Jackie Marquette, educator, author, and parent of adult son with autism

"Kathy Deyer Bolduc offers a moving and inspiring account of life with Joel. She is courageous and honest in sharing the love and anger provoked by life with a severely autistic son. Kathy shares with us the reality of Joel's surprising giftedness and her reliance upon the love of Jesus for her and for Joel." —Jean Vanier, founder, L'Arche Communities

autism
& alleluias

Kathleen Deyer Bolduc
Foreword by Bill Gaventa

JUDSON PRESS
PUBLISHERS SINCE 1824
VALLEY FORGE, PA

Autism & Alleluias
© 2010 by Kathleen Deyer Bolduc
All rights reserved.

Unless otherwise noted, Bible quotations in this volume are from the Revised Standard Version of the Bible, copyright © 1946, 1952, 1971, by the Division of Christian Education of the National Council of the Churches of Christ in the U.S.A. Used by permission.

Quotations marked The Message are from THE MESSAGE. Copyright © 1993, 1994, 1995. Used by permission of NavPress Publishing Group.

"For Me" first appeared in *A Place Called Acceptance: Ministry with Families of Children with Disabilities* © 2000 Kathleen Deyer Bolduc.

The Haworth Press, Inc., Binghamton, NY, Journal of Religion, Disability & Health, "Embracing our Brokenness: Poems and Reflections on Disability and the Kingdom," Vol. 4, Number 4, 2001, p. 65.

The poems that were included in that article were:
"Immersion"
"Waiting Rooms"
"Emmaus Eyes"
"Pearl Beyond Price"

Library of Congress Cataloging-in-Publication Data

Bolduc, Kathleen Deyer, 1952-
  Autism & alleluias / Kathleen Deyer Bolduc ; foreword by Bill Gaventa. -- 1st ed.
    p. cm.
  ISBN 978-0-8170-1568-8 (pbk. : alk. paper) 1. Bolduc, Joel--Mental health. 2. Autistic children--United States--Biography. 3. Autism--Religious aspects--Christianity. I. Title. II. Title: Autism and alleluias.

  RJ506.A9B643 2010
  618.92'858820092--dc22
  [B]

                                    2009045624

Printed in the U.S.A.

First Edition, 2010.

Contents

Foreword
Helping Us Find Our Psalms

I remember that as a child growing up in a very religious environment, with lots of Sunday school classes, Bible studies, and general encouragement of Bible reading, the psalms were not my favorite part of Scripture. They were too abstract. I wanted story. Journeys. Battles. History. Not prayers, long or short. Not words that sounded sometimes like the songs we sang in worship, sometimes not. They were just boring.

But then, as an adult, I began to have my own stories. My own struggles. My own questions. My own discoveries. My own affirmations. I found my calling in a place I might have least expected, listening to and working with people with developmental disabilities and their families. Over and over again, I heard their stories, but even more importantly I had experience after experience, time after time, when insight and revelation broke into my spirit in ever new ways, or one might say, in ancient ways that led me back to those symbols and stories in my biblical foundations. Those symbols and stories now helped me understand both my own experience and passage after passage of Scripture in ways I had never anticipated. With every height of excitement, discovery, and appreciation, and every low of frustration, despair, and even depression, I began to read the psalms in new ways. Like countless generations before me, I found every single feeling and revelation there, waiting to help me interpret my story.

What Kathy Bolduc has done in this volume is to write a book of modern day psalms. Some are her own poems and read like psalms of old. But she does for us what the psalmists did not: she invites us into the concrete, messy, detailed, and often colorful experiences of her life with Joel, her son with autism. She shares her stories, and then lets us see the ways her questions, faith, hopes, and, finally, love, left her open to finding and seeing God in the places, events, and relationships where she, and we the readers, might least expect.

Unlike the ancient psalmists, she lets us into the specific story behind each revelation and praise. The stories share the journey through Joel's adolescence until his launch into adulthood, but her prayers, stories, and connections of her story with Bible story are not about linear time, but about God's time and places, rhythms of life beyond our control, valleys and mountaintops we usually seek to avoid in our preference for predictability and order.

Readers of faith who are parents or friends of people with developmental disabilities will see and read themselves into many of these stories. But even more importantly, Kathy Bolduc is inviting everyone, familiar with disability and Scripture or not, to take a look at the heights and depths of our questions, pain, and joys, and join her in using ancient words to understand, appreciate, and even give praise for, the unexpected gifts and fullness of our lives.

Bill Gaventa, MDiv
Editor, *Journal of Religion, Disability and Health*

Acknowledgments

It took so long to birth this book—eight long years—that there is no possible way to acknowledge everyone who had a hand in its delivery. Without the following people, however, I doubt it would have seen the light of day. I would like to thank:

Cassandra Williams, editor extraordinaire, tireless advocate, and coach.

The Poor Clares of Cincinnati, whose gift for hospitality is unsurpassed. Much of this book was written within the peaceful walls of their monastery in Winton Woods.

The Ursulines of Brown County, who gifted me with the perfect place, Springer House, to finish this manuscript.

Patty Kyrlach, critique partner and monastery buddy.

Jackie Eyre, accountability partner and fellow dreamer.

My contemplative prayer group—Cheryl, Mary Sue, and Jackie—in whose presence, in the silence, I heard God's still, small, yet very authoritative voice, saying, "Finish the book, Kathy."

The friends of my Tuesday night small group, who have surrounded my family with years of soaking prayer

The women of the Red Tent for all those years of listening.

Annette and Ed Eckert, for laughter, friendship, and unwavering prayer support.

My sons Matt and Justin, and daughter-in-law, Elizabeth, for lighting up my life, and for loving me just the way I am.

My husband, Wally, companion in Christ and love of my life.

And last, but certainly not least, the subject of this book, Joel Christopher Bolduc, whose very life is a testimony to God's presence among us.

Introduction

The LORD will fulfil his purpose for [my son];
thy steadfast love, O LORD, endures for ever.
—Psalm 138:8

If you are reading this book, chances are that you are the parent, grandparent, aunt, uncle, or sibling of a child (or adult) with autism. Or maybe someone in your church fellowship has autism, or you work with children with disabilities. Perhaps the title, with its use of the word "alleluias" in conjunction with the word "autism," piqued your curiosity.

If you are living with autism, or know someone who is, you know just how difficult day-to-day life can be. I certainly do. My youngest son, Joel, who is now 24 years old, has autism, intellectual disabilities, and an anxiety disorder. While I love Joel deeply, I can relate to the famous first line from M. Scott Peck's book, *The Road Less Traveled:* "Life is difficult."

Joel's neurological disabilities have caused behaviors over the years that have been extremely difficult to deal with—aggression, tantrums, manic swings, sleepless nights, an inability to be in large groups of people or to tolerate certain noises. His intellectual disabilities have made learning the easiest of tasks difficult. He cannot read, do simple math, tie his shoes, or ride a two-wheel bike. Everything I had valued in my life before Joel's birth—intelligence, efficiency, logic, self-control—had to be re-thought and re-valued.

So, where do the *alleluias* fit in?

Someone once said, "Pain is where we meet God face to face." I can say, without a moment's hesitation, that through Joel, through autism, I have not only met, but come to know God on a first-name basis.

This is not a book about a parent's immersion in autism research. This is not a book about a child's recovery from autism. As a matter of fact, you will find next to nothing about the thousands of hours and dollars we have spent on physical therapy, occupational therapy, speech therapy, play therapy, sensory integration training, music therapy, individual therapy, or marriage therapy within the pages of this book. This doesn't mean they weren't necessary, helpful, or important. They were. They just aren't the focus of this story.

While *His Name is Joel: Searching for God in a Son's Disability* was about my journey through grief toward a place called acceptance, this book is a love story. It is a story of God's unconditional love, acceptance, and unwavering presence, and the many ways in which God mediates that love, in our little corner of the world, through Joel, who just happens to have autism.

My hope is that our story will resonate with your story and that you will meet God face to face on your walk with autism as well.

Alleluia!

Immersion

Seduced by myths
of the effortless life
I float, footless,
into adulthood,
down streets of dreams—
love,
marriage,
motherhood,
happily ever after

Until a broken boy
lays waste to legends.
Dear God, the shock of it,
the plunge,
the headlong speed of it,
the darkness,
the fear,
wind whistling in ears,
and louder still
the roar of a river,
rising to meet my fall.

The impact rude, cold.
The unimaginable strength of it,
the mighty, weighty pull of it!
I flail for bearings,
for surface, for breath

Until

A hint of buoyancy,
a whisper of weightlessness,
a sense of sufficiency
(not in myself,
but in the river's adequacy)
rises within.

As the thought, trust,
flowers,
my flailing form shoots
to the surface;
an otter, sleek
and substantial, swimming
with my son,
the broken one,
he, too, glossy and gorgeous
and awesomely made.

Embraced,
enveloped,
enfolded,
upheld,
not in the stuff of fairy tales,
but in the waters
of life itself.

For Me!

For now we see in a mirror dimly, but then face to face.
Now I know in part; then I shall understand fully,
even as I have been fully understood.
—*1 Corinthians 13:12*

It is Communion Sunday. Joel, eleven, sits between his father, Wally, and me. As usual, we are sitting in the front pew so that Joel can't kick the pew in front of us or reach forward and grab someone's hair. By trial and error we have found that with Dad to his right, Mom to his left, and empty space to the front, Joel can usually sit through half of the worship service without too much fidgeting.

We have temporarily given up on Sunday school. Sunday school is just too difficult—too much like "real" school, a place where "keeping it together" is a constant struggle. Because Joel loves music and is enthralled by the choir, the beginning of the service is something he looks forward to.

Often he stands up, pretend baton in hand, and imitates the choir director. During hymns he loves to sing along, usually (thank God) in tune, with a few words right, and always with a loud *amen!* at the end, generally a few beats behind the rest of the congregation.

During the boring parts of the service (any part without music is boring as far as Joel is concerned), he twists and turns in the pew, stares at the people behind us, waves at the pastor, swings his feet, claps his hands or stomps his feet (he usually saves these last two for times of silent prayer), and at least once during every service says in a loud voice, "I have to go to the bathroom!" Worshiping with Joel is an interesting experience. It's not unlike sitting on the edge of your seat during an action movie, when you're not quite sure what's going to happen next—you only know *something* is going to happen. It's difficult to develop a prayerful attitude in those circumstances.

On the first Sunday of the month, Communion is served. We pass the bread along the pews, administering it to one another, saying, "This is the body of Jesus, broken for you." Likewise, we pass the wine to one another with the words, "This is Jesus' blood, shed that you might live." Wally and I allow Joel to take a piece of bread, reciting the familiar words to which he never seems to pay attention. He chews the bread, picking at the sticky stuff left in his teeth with his fingers, but far prefers the wine, which in our church is really grape juice. Again, we recite the words to him. "Joel, this is Jesus' blood, shed for you." He slurps down the juice and sticks his tongue into the cup, determined to get every last drop. His father and I close our eyes briefly to pray our own private prayers of thanksgiving for this unbelievable gift of grace. Joel cranes his neck to watch as everyone else is served, and wiggles through the remaining quiet time.

This particular Sunday, the pastor raises the plate high in the air and proclaims, "This is the body of Christ, broken for you." Then he raises the cup, saying, "And this is the blood of Christ, poured out that you might live." Joel pulls on my sleeve. I look down to see him grinning, his face lit up as if from within. He stands up tall, and taps himself on his chest.

"For *me*! For *me*!" he cries joyfully. He turns around to the people behind us. "For *me*!" he repeats. "For *me*!"

Ordinary time stops. All that exists in this moment is the radiant look of understanding on Joel's face. Joel *knows* that God loves him. On a spiritual level he also *knows* that God has sent Jesus for him. My body remains in the front pew of College Hill Presbyterian Church, but my spirit stands in the sacred presence of God. All the accumulated Sunday hours of embarrassment, impatience, frustration, disapointment, and yearning for wholeness as the world knows wholeness slough away as I watch the love of God glimmer like gold in the face of my son.

Prayer

Lord, for a moment today, the mirror of existence, like a mirror wiped clear of steam, brightened and cleared, and I understood clearly. Joel, despite his disabilities, is spiritually whole. I glimpsed a realm of existence where schedules and priorities and developmental timetables do not exist. A realm where it is enough simply "to be." I praise you, Lord, for letting my son teach me this truth. Amen.

All You Need Is Love

God is love, and he who abides in love abides in God, and God abides in him. In this is love perfected with us, that we may have confidence for the day of judgment, because as he is so are we in this world. There is no fear in love, but perfect love casts out fear.

—1 John 4:16–18

"My papa died. I miss my papa. Do you miss Papa? My dad's sad. Papa died."

Joel, the son I thought would never talk, cannot stop talking about his papa. Wally's father passed away six months ago. The whole family grieves, but Joel's grief is by far the most transparent.

"Yes, Joel, I miss Papa too. But today we're visiting Grandma Barb. Did you bring your picture album? Grandma likes it when you share your pictures with her."

Distracted from his Papa-talk for a moment, Joel pulls one of his many picture albums out of his backpack and flips through the pages. In the meantime, my mind spins through one memory movie after another. Dad walking into the house and yelling, "Play me a song on that piano, Kate!" Dad in his apron, making French crepes filled with raspberry jam and sprinkled with powdered sugar. Piling the boys into Dad's '61 convertible for a drive through the park. The countless hours Mom and I spent together—the diet classes, the decorating, the hours browsing through antique shops.

Gone. All gone.

We pull into the parking lot of the Alzheimer center where Wally's mother now lives. Dad cared for Mom at home for years before it got too hard—before she needed professional care. Less than a year later he died unexpectedly of a massive heart attack, on his way home from vacation. None of us could wrap our minds around it, the fact that Dad was gone; the fact that Mom no longer knew her children and grandchildren.

Walking up to the front door of Mom's building, I let Joel ring the bell. Once buzzed in, we enter the spacious lobby, which is tastefully decorated in shades of rose and green. Warm lamplight brightens the dimness of late afternoon. As pretty as the setting is, it cannot hide the smells of a nursing home. The odors of urine and dinner compete for attention. My nose wrinkles, and I attempt to hold my breath.

"Hamburgers," Joel says, sniffing.

"Mmmhmmm," I mutter.

As we walk down the hallway toward Mom's room, several women in wheelchairs reach out toward Joel. It's like running the gauntlet. On our twice-weekly trips here, Joel is hugged several times before we make it to Grandma's room. I am amazed each time at his equanimity with the situation, considering that he rarely lets people outside the family into his personal space.

Mom's door is open. The room is dark, the curtains pulled tight. She is napping in the antique rocking chair we brought from her home. We've worked hard to make her room as home-like as possible. Family pictures cover the top of a Victorian dresser from her bedroom at home, and artwork she and Dad collected over the years decorates the walls. I walk over to the window and open the blinds. Joel approaches his grandma.

"Pictures!" he says, waking her. I walk to her side and lean down, giving her a kiss.

As usual, she is first confused and then delighted to see us, even though she doesn't recognize us. It is getting harder and harder to find the "real" Barb when we visit. The mother-in-law whom I knew and loved for twenty-some years was a highly intelligent woman, a fastidious dresser, always impeccably groomed. Today she can barely string together a sentence, her sweatshirt is stained, and there are hairs growing out of her chin. I make note to speak to the nurse.

But Joel doesn't seem to notice. At eleven, he's still not too big to sit on his grandma's lap and share pictures of his brothers, of his mom and dad, of his black lab, Poco. Mom points to each one and makes comments, none of them making much sense, but that doesn't bother Joel. He knows he is making his grandma happy, and that's just fine with him.

Suddenly it strikes me—the different lenses through which my son and I view this more-than-difficult family situation.

I smell urine. He smells hamburger.

I see strangers invading my son's personal space. He invites their touch.

I am immersed in a world of old memories. He is making new memories.

I grieve for the mother-in-law I once knew. He plays with the grandma who is here today.

Wally's sister and I have spent a lot of time talking about Alzheimer's, this terrible disease that robs people of their memory, their personality, their dignity. What happens to a person as memory fades away? Are they still "there"? Does their "spirit" go somewhere else? Exactly who resides in this shell of a person who in no way resembles the woman or man we used to know?

Joel doesn't have the IQ to ask these questions, but perhaps he doesn't ask them simply because there is no doubt in his mind. This is Grandma Barb. Papa is gone, and Joel misses him and talks about him every day. But Grandma is here, now, in this place that smells like hamburgers, in this place where everyone is glad to see him. Grandma holds him on her lap and looks at his pictures. She loves him and he loves her.

In Joel's world, that's all that counts.

Prayer

Lord, I will never forget these last days with Mom. With Joel beside me, what seems unbearable becomes bearable. How awesome to watch him connect on a spiritual level with the woman I love but no longer recognize. Thank you for Joel's presence in this place. Thank you for his model of unconditional love, and for the way he encourages me to change my lenses so that I might look back at these moments with love instead of fear and despair. Amen.

God of Heaven, Asleep in Straw

He is the image of the invisible God, the first-born of all creation; for in him all things were created, in heaven and on earth, visible and invisible . . . for in him all the fullness of God was pleased to dwell.
—*Colossians 1:15a, 19*

Christmas Eve. Candlelight service. My mother, husband, three sons, and I duck into the church, shaking rain off our coats, anticipating a joyful celebration. The sanctuary glows in the light of a hundred candles, their soft light glimmering, throwing shadows on the walls. We find a pew near the front and pile in. The atmosphere is hushed, pregnant with expectation. Many sit in an attitude of prayer, while others whisper quietly.

Joel wriggles out of his coat. "Church is over! Wanna donut!" he says loudly.

"Shhh," I warn, holding a finger to my lips. Heads turn in our direction. "We're here to praise God for baby Jesus. No donuts tonight."

A young tenor stands and sings the poignant "In the Bleak Midwinter." His voice, pure and beautiful, rises through space like the voice of an angel.

"Hungry! Wanna eat!" Joel's twelve-year-old face, still pudgy with baby fat, is set in an expression I know too well. We're in for trouble.

Several people look toward us. Are they frowning? I want to crawl under the pew, but simply hold my finger to my lips once more. Joel fidgets through the processional hymn, and continues to chatter about donuts as the pastor reads the first lesson from Scripture. My mother rolls her eyes. My husband grits his teeth. Joel's big brothers, Matt and Justin, make goofy faces, trying to distract him, to no avail. Joel is fixated on donuts and there is no diverting him.

Oh, Lord, it's impossible to worship with this child. Can't he be quiet and sit still just this once? It's Christmas Eve! It's time for wonder and awe and quiet contemplation, not for squirming and fidgeting and talking about donuts!

The answer comes before I open my eyes.

Yes, Kathy, it is Christmas Eve. You're here to celebrate the birth of my son. Remember the words you memorized as a child? "And this will be a sign for you; you will find a babe wrapped in swaddling cloths and lying in a manger." Think about it. God of heaven, asleep in straw.

As the words fade, my eyes take in the altar, the mass of red poinsettias, the flickering candlelight, the quiet faces of well-dressed people. But my inner eye sees a rude stable, carved out of rock. There, too, the light of a flame flickers. The stable is cold and damp. The smell of wet animal and dung is overpowering. The straw lies trampled and dirty, the mother exhausted, the father concerned. The babe cries a lusty cry before suckling at his mother's breast. A cow lows as wind whistles through the cave's opening, stirring dust and straw that tickle the nose and sting the eye. Shepherds, rough and unkempt, jostle their way to the babe's bed, bending their knees in worship. Loud alleluias fill the sky as the cave glows with an unearthly light.

Miracle of miracles. God become human. Perfect power, exposed and vulnerable. God, the very God who fashioned the universe, choosing to take on the disability of human form.

My yearning for the "perfect" Christmas Eve fades away. I put my arm around Joel and kiss his head.

"Donuts," he says again.

"We'll eat when we get home," I whisper into his ear. "Right now, let's sing real loud and worship Jesus." Joel looks up at me and smiles at my change in attitude. As we stand to sing "O Come All Ye Faithful," his voice, slightly off-key, carries above all the rest.

Prayer

Oh Lord, how much you must love us! You, in whom all the fullness of God does dwell, taking on the confines of human form. You know what it is to be cold and hungry. You know what it is to grieve. You know what it is to be disabled. Thank you, God, for the gift of your son. And thank you for the gift of my sons, who teach me daily about what it means to be human; what it means to love unconditionally. Amen.

Meltdown

Be angry, but sin not; commune with your own hearts on your beds,
and be silent. Offer right sacrifices, and put your trust in the Lord.
—Psalm 4:4

I fly into the school parking lot, a smoldering rage burning within my chest.

Joel's teacher has called me again. She calls me daily:

"Mrs. Bolduc, we need you here to help calm Joel."

I've spent spend more time in Joel's classroom this year than at home, where I work.

Anger, tamped down for months, broke the surface with today's call.

"Mrs. Bolduc, Joel is in the principal's office. We've had him in a hold for twenty minutes, and he's just now beginning to settle down. Please come pick him up."

I enter the principal's office to find Joel subdued, surrounded by the principal, the teacher, and a teacher's aide. His face is blotchy, his hair darkened by sweat, his chest heaving. I hold my arms open and he runs to me.

"Twenty minutes, Mrs. Bolduc, with two adults restraining him so that he couldn't hurt himself or others. Please take him home. We'll call and let you know when he can return."

Disbelief. Anger. Bitterness.

We had moved thirteen-year-old Joel to this school in the fall because this particular teacher was trained in autism.

Her classroom was run with a high degree of structure and creativity. And yet my son was an enigma to her.

When I had suggested we bring in a county team of behavioral specialists we'd worked with the previous year at a different school, the teacher refused, convincing the IEP team that we did not need outside intervention. And now this? Twenty minutes of restraint?

Panic. Helplessness. Fury.

These people are professionals, and they have no idea how to help my son?

I'm not an autism expert. We only received this autism diagnosis a few months ago. For years his diagnosis was "moderate mental retardation." I'm just a mother. I spend countless hours each week ferrying Joel from therapist to therapist, specialist to specialist. Caring for Joel is my daily food, morning, noon, and night. I can't sleep. I can't write. I'm neglecting Matt and Justin. My marriage is suffering. I count on the school to educate my son, and to help me learn ways to teach him at home.

These people are professionals, and they have no idea how to help my son?

I am speechless in the face of this ineptitude. Without thought, running on sheer emotion, I grab Joel's hand and walk out of the principal's office. I help Joel climb into the van and drive 40 mph through a 25 mph zone to the school district's administration building. I fly up the driveway, a scream building inside of me. My head tells me to turn around and go home, to come back when I'm calmer, but my gut urges me on. I am a mother bear defending her cub.

Joel sits wide-eyed in the back seat. His meltdown has worn him out, so he is quiet, waiting to see what will happen. I careen into a parking space and jump out of the van. I open the back door and wait for Joel to climb out. I march into the building, Joel following behind. I yank open the door. The secretary, whose son played soccer with Joel's big brother, Justin, smiles.

"Kathy!" Her smile quickly vanishes when she sees the look on my face.

"What can I do for you?" she asks.

"Ann Hart," I answer, my teeth clenched.

"I'm sorry, but Ann is out on an appointment. Do you want to leave a message?"

"No!" I fairly spit the word, turn on my heel, and head for the van, Joel caught in the tailwind of my fury.

I wait while Joel climbs in and buckles his seat belt. I shove the gear stick into reverse and back up full speed. Yanking it into drive, I roar down the long driveway, my heart thudding. I'm having trouble breathing.

A car approaches before we reach the end of the drive. The driver's eyes meet mine for a split second. It's Ann. I slam on the brakes and put the van in reverse. Ann has stopped her car. This is a woman we've worked with since Joel was in preschool. As the Director of Special Services she has always seemed to have Joel's best interests at heart. I've come to trust her. I like to think we have some kind of relationship. Our cars pull parallel to one another. Her face is wrinkled with astonishment. Suddenly, I am aware that I must look like a woman suffering a psychotic break.

"Kathy," she says as she rolls down her window. "What's wrong?"

"What's wrong is everything!" I shout. My face twists, trying to hold back the tears. "Joel's teacher is supposed to be an expert in autism. But Joel's behavior keeps getting worse and worse. She expects me to be there every day. They had him in a hold today for twenty minutes! And you ask what's wrong? What's going on here? What are they doing to my child?"

Ann listens until I finish.

"You're right, Kathy. We need to do something. This can't be good for Joel. Or for you. I'll look into it. Why don't you go home and rest?"

I laugh, hysterically.

"Kathy, listen to me. Go home and call your husband. You need to rest. I'm serious."

I nod my head. Like Joel, I'm spent from my meltdown. I drive home slowly, my head numb. I pull into the driveway, wait until Joel climbs out of the car, walk up the porch steps, unlock the door, and pick up the phone.

"Wally. I need you. Please come home."

Prayer

Lord, why do I judge my anger? Why do I swallow it, go about my days while it churns in my belly like undigested food? Teach me to acknowledge my anger—to deal with it before it crescendos to impotent rage. Let my anger at the system be righteous anger—anger that motivates change—anger that results in a better life for my son. Amen.

Waiting Rooms

I spend so many hours
in waiting rooms
pediatrician, neurologist
behavioral specialist, psychiatrist
school psychologist, play therapist
so many doctors
so much advice
so little understanding
What do they know
(despite diplomas
on sterile walls)
of living with disability?

It's different here
This therapist knows disability
It moved in twenty-some years ago
with her firstborn child
She plays with my son
leaving me alone
with a cup of tea, my thoughts, and magazines

Travel & Leisure, Smithsonian, Family Fun
Sometimes I read them and fume
What happened to my family's fun?
Only the beach for us
familiar and undemanding
No museums or theme parks
too stimulating
No long road trips stopping
at motels with pools each night
too disruptive

Above the magazine rack
brochures offer a better life
Women's Mind-Body Wellness,
Natural Wellness & Healing
Conflict Management
I hear my son's laughter
the sound of knocking on flimsy walls
his current game, sometimes funny
sometimes enough to make me scream stop

I sip raspberry tea
and step into Monet's garden
onto a bridge awash
in a dream of green
countless scenes of beauty
just outside the cottage door
waiting for the artist's brush

I wonder
Can I carve a garden
from the weedy turf of life
plant colors of my choosing
in arrangements pleasing to my eye
weed out thistles
of resentment and fear
replace them with flowers
of joy and contentment?

Suspended between past and future
in this waiting room
today
I weave a garden plan of beauty
while I wait
for my son

The Band-Aid

Peace I leave with you; my peace I give to you; not as the world gives do I give to you. Let not your hearts be troubled, neither let them be afraid.
—John 14:27

I sit in the wingback chair beside the front window, tensing and relaxing each major muscle group, willing my body to let go of the tension that has been steadily building like steam in a pressure cooker. Once a teacher of Christian meditation and relaxation techniques, I've come to a place where relaxation is a forgotten art. I close my eyes and attempt to center down in prayer. Instead, a whining, petulant five-year-old surfaces from within me, shaking her fist at God.

Lord, I can't face another school year like the last one. I can't! I won't! Deep into the dog days of August, school looms just ahead, and like the thunderheads gathering outside the window, it threatens heavy weather.

Visions of last year's monthly behavior meetings float before my mind's eye. Six, seven, eight people crowded around a table in the school's conference room. Sheets of behavior data passed from hand to hand. The days of Joel's thirteenth year charted and graphed and printed out in full color for all to see, analyze, and discuss. Some months' data showed up to fifty aggressive incidents per day. Hair-pulling, kicking, hitting, cussing, and yanking glasses off peoples' faces. The graphs showed a definite cycle. Four fairly calm weeks, followed by two weeks of intense agitation and aggression. Month after month it remained the same, regardless of positive interventions, consequences, staff changes, medication changes.

It is the same at home; four good weeks followed by two intense weeks of disrupted sleep, constant motion, tantrums, and aggression. Continually on guard, I watch my son intensely, anticipating every move, reading his moods like an investor watches the stock market. Support staff comes and goes, only the hardiest few—those with a true sense of commitment—hanging on for the rough ride. Exhaustion is my constant companion.

The querulous five-year-old quits shaking her fist and crumples in a dejected heap.

I can't do it anymore, Lord. You take him. He's all yours.

No sooner has the thought crossed my mind than a golden light, pulsing and alive, fills the darkness behind my closed eyelids and then floods my entire frame—my exhausted, depleted frame—warming, renewing, re-creating. As quickly as it appears the light is gone, only to be followed by an intense silence, louder than any human word or sound. The parched ground of my being opens itself fully to the Spirit's life-giving waters.

The thud of the mailbox closing outside my window breaks my meditation. I reluctantly rise and stretch before opening the front door to scoop up the mail.

I stand on the porch in the storm-charged air and absentmindedly flip through the envelopes. A handwritten address among the junk mail and bills catches my attention. Sister Mary Grace! Her friendship is one of the blessings I've received since the publication of my first book, *His Name is Joel: Searching for God in a Son's Disability.*

A Dominican nun I'd met through the mail some months earlier, she is a talented artist with a heart for people with disabilities. She had written to thank me for sharing my struggle to find God's special gift in Joel, and went on to write in her first letter, "I'm interested in doing something with that dream you had of the children surrounding Jesus and Joel putting a Band-Aid (on the wound of the nail?!) How powerful." Since then we've corresponded regularly, and I was privileged to meet her in person when I traveled to a conference in Washington DC, where her monastery is located.

Thunder mutters overhead as I open the envelope, and a gust of wind catches the tri-folded letter, sweeping a photograph to the ground. Hurriedly, I run into the yard to retrieve it. She has finished the painting! In the center is Jesus, his head encircled by a glow of golden light, surrounded by a group of children with various disabilities—autism, cerebral palsy, seizure disorders—and kneeling next to him, placing a Band-Aid onto his wounded hand, is Joel.

I hold in my hand an artist's rendition of my vision—Jesus in the middle of Joel's classroom. Jesus who has been present with Joel all along. Jesus who promises to walk with Joel into this year's classroom. Jesus who will be present with Joel. Always. No matter the outer circumstances of Joel's life. No matter the behaviors. No matter the level of agitation. I hold in my hands the visual promise that Jesus will be there.

As I look at Joel placing that Band-Aid with such care and concentration onto Jesus' wounded and resurrected body, I know there is no pain, no humiliation, no anxiety or fear that Jesus himself has not faced in his time here on earth.

I lift my eyes to the sky. Roiling black clouds have rendered mid-afternoon near night. I stand for several moments, watching the trees dance and bow in the gusting wind. A bolt of lightning hits in the woods behind the house, answered by an immediate crash of thunder.

I turn and open the door, my spirit singing a song of peace.

Prayer
I praise you, Lord, for your promised presence. Thank you for this concrete reminder that no matter the outer circumstances of Joel's life, you are there with him. Amen.

We Need Jesus!

At that time Jesus declared, "I thank thee, Father, Lord of heaven and earth, that thou hast hidden these things from the wise and understanding and revealed them to babes."
—Matthew 11:25

It's Tuesday morning, 7:15. Wally was up hours ago and has already left for work, and after a night of tossing and turning I'm hoping to sleep in until 8:00.

Joel's feet hit the floor with a thud, and I pull the pillow over my head against the loud bang of his door hitting the wall, as it does every morning. Then, the slam of the bathroom door, the crash of the toilet seat lid, and a few moments later, 170 pounds of fourteen-year-old boy jumping on my bed. Ouch!

Fifteen minutes later, Joel is ready to roll. Never mind that he's pajama-clad and barefoot. Never mind that it is 38 degrees with a wind chill way below freezing. Never mind that I am nowhere near awake. Before I have the coffee started, Joel is standing in the front yard, checking the sky for rain or snow.

I poke my head out the door. "Get in here! It's freezing!"

A school bus lumbers by and wheezes to a stop in front of the neighbor's house.

"Bus?" Joel asks, suddenly anxious.

"Not your bus," I answer. "Remember? Today is Tuesday. You go to the Fairfield Center and work on Tuesday."

He follows me into the house.

"No school today. Center. Time to go."

Anxiety oozes out of his voice. I can hear it. And I haven't even had a cup of coffee yet. Not a good sign.

"No Joel. On Tuesday I drive you to the center at 9:30. It's only 7:30. That's two hours away. How about a bowl of cereal?"

"No! Wanna go outside! Wanna go *now*!" He rushes to the door and runs outside.

I dash upstairs to get dressed, first yelling out the door.

I finally talk him into coming inside. His size-ten feet are red with cold. It takes fifteen minutes to talk him into going upstairs to get dressed. Another ten to get dressed. Another five to get him washed up. Joel's anxiety level, as well as mine, is now through the roof.

I somehow keep my cool, vital to keeping him from totally losing it. But when it comes to putting on his shoes he starts grabbing for my glasses, something he does when the anxiety is really high. *Don't overreact. Remain calm. Quietly tell him to put his hands down.*

I'm a human being. Some days this just isn't possible.

"Stop it!" I hiss. "Quit grabbing at me!"

That's all it takes. His face turns bright red. His arms start flailing, lashing out at me. Cuss words, words he never uses unless extremely agitated, dirty the air. A full-blown anxiety attack and it's only 8 a.m. I somehow manage to get his shoes on without losing my glasses.

"Get in the car," I command. "We'll go get bagels."

No deal. He won't get near the car. He's too big for me to take by the hand or lead by the shoulder. If I can't talk him into doing something, there's absolutely no doing it.

"No work! Stay home today!"

I know the routine. He'll be impossible to deal with for up to an hour. He's been disintegrating like this nearly every day for the past couple of months, but usually *later* in the day.

I am tired. Exceedingly tired. I don't know how much longer I can do this. I go into the house, sit down on the couch, and cry.

Hearing me, Joel follows me in. He sits down next to me and reaches a hand toward my face, this time to pat my face rather than to grab.

"Mom's crying," he says.

I cannot answer. He's quiet for a moment.

"We need Jesus," he says, patting my shoulder. "We need Jesus."

Joel remains calm while we finish getting ready, and I am able to drive him to work at 9:30.

Living with disability is never easy; it's just that some days are more difficult than others. I find myself crying off and on throughout the day. But even as the tears fall, Joel's wise words echo through my heart.

We need Jesus.

Yes, Joel. We need Jesus. Thanks for reminding me.

Prayer

Lord, so often I forget to call your name in the midst of the storms. I praise you for Joel's words of wisdom today. Teach me to listen to him more often, for he has much to teach me. Amen.

You Are Enough

*For thou didst form my inward parts, thou didst knit me together
in my mother's womb ... thy eyes beheld my unformed substance;
in thy book were written every one of them, the days that were
formed for me, when as yet there was none of them.*
—Psalm 139:13, 16

The afternoon stretches out in front of me, luxuriously empty.
I've come a day early to attend a healing prayer conference,
led by Francis McNutt. I need this time alone as much as I
need the healing touch of prayer.

You're not enough, a voice has been telling me. *You're not
enough as a mother to Matt and Justin. You're certainly not
enough as a mother to Joel. You're not enough as a wife to
Wally. You can't get it right. You'll never get it right. Admit
it. You're not enough. You'll never be enough.*

I recognize the voice. I've heard it throughout my life.
Intellectually, I know I should ignore it. Spiritually, I know I
should pray against it. Emotionally, I agree with it. All I have
to do is look around at my life. I can't make things better for
Joel—I can't find the right doctors, the right therapies, the
right school, the right behavior plan.

After taking care of Joel's needs, I have precious little
energy left over for Matt and Justin. I attend their school
concerts, the soccer games, the piano recitals, the teacher
conferences, but only part of me is there.

And my marriage? An even smaller part of me is showing
up for Wally. I'm not sure where the rest of me is. The "not

enough" part of me has succumbed to mind-numbing fatigue. But I keep on slogging through the wet cement of my days, because that is what you do.

I don't know who I am anymore.

I settle into my hotel room, grateful for its anonymity, its lack of family pictures and scattered toys, shoes, and laundry. I lie down on the bed and read for an hour—McNutt's book, *Healing Prayer.* I look up some of the Scriptures he cites. I am nervous about the prayer conference tomorrow. *Does it truly happen? Does God still heal today? Do miracles still happen? Will I be caught up in some kind of ecstasy? Speak in tongues? Lose control? Oh Lord, don't let me lose control. I've been working so very hard to stay in control. I don't want to lose the little bit of me that is left.*

I close my eyes to meditate, repeating my centering word in my mind. *Maranatha. Come Lord Jesus. Maranatha. Maranatha.*

Breathing deep from my diaphragm, I let my breath and the words wash over me. Gradually, my stiff muscles begin to soften. A thought floats through my mind—*a person can only live with chronic stress for so long before it begins impacting the physical body.* I bring my mind back to my centering words.

Maranatha. Come Lord Jesus. Maranatha. Maranatha.

I sit for what seems like hours. Images swirl. Joel's upcoming birthday party at school. His last IEP meeting, where I rushed out of the room in tears. Justin's rebellion over doing his homework. Matt's upcoming French test, the one he needs to ace to pass the course. The camping trip Joel took with his class, the one he'd been so excited about, and the phone call the next day saying to come and get him, that he was out of control. I let each image pass like scenes on a movie screen, not holding on to them, simply noticing them and letting them go.

Maranatha. Come Lord Jesus. Maranatha. Maranatha.

Gradually, a deep peace wells up in my chest, and with it all images disappear. A river of peace flows through my body. I feel heavy and buoyant at the same time. My field of vision shimmers with a bright, golden light. Out of the silence comes a voice—a voice distinctively different from the "you're not enough" voice.

Kathy, I want you to know, down to the deepest part of you, down to your very bones, that you are who I made you to be. Your very footprint was fashioned by me, and in my book are written all the days of your life.

Wave after wave of love washes over me, cleansing, restoring, energizing. An image of my birth certificate rises up—my tiny, newborn footprint in black ink, the one-of-a-kind whorls of my little toes and heel clearly marked. I am rooted in time and space by that footprint. That footprint was fashioned by God.

I am God's creation. I am God's beloved daughter. I am enough. I am more than enough.

The healing conference does not start until tomorrow, but the healing has already begun. The lie—*I am not enough*—has been pulled up by the roots and thrown away. I will take my prayer requests for Joel with me tomorrow—prayers for peace to replace his anxiety, for brain chemicals to come into divine alignment, for the right doctors and therapists and teachers and friends to come alongside us. But I now know, deep in my bones, that I am loved; that Joel is loved; that Wally, Matt, and Justin are loved; that we are God's beloved sons and daughters, no matter the outward circumstances of our lives.

Together, with Christ, we are enough.

Prayer

O Lord, what a gift you've given me. The gift of your love, freely given. The gift of your presence, fully experienced. The gift of your truth, finally heard. Alleluia! Amen.

On Being Pruned

I
Abandoned shoe,
crumpled, gray,
tire treads branding sole.
Ridiculous,
the decision to retrieve it.

II
Funny it should be a shoe,
of all things, thrown
from support staff's car
earlier that day.
Shoes a symbol that stalks me in sleep,
dream after dream of baby shoes,
buried shoes, lost shoes.
This shoe, a Nike,
all too real.

III
Three generations,
me and my mother in front,
the perpetrator, Joel, in back,
slowly cruise construction zone.
Highway narrows to one lane,
concrete barriers loom left and right,
impatient drivers gesture in rearview mirror.
Pulling over at end of entrance ramp,
I put car in park, jump out, slam door,
wait for hole in traffic, dash across highway,
risk lives, three lives,
for a shoe!

IV
Good mothers do not leave
$70.00 Nikes on highway berms.
Good mother's sons never
throw shoes from speeding cars.
Good mother's sons have words
for anxiety, anger, boredom, fear.
Good mother's lives are fresh-scrubbed and clean
like their children's faces,
never smeared, like mine, with spaghetti sauce
or mustard or, God-forbid, tire treads.

V

Cradled on a mother's lap,
I am barefoot, sweaty, inconsolable
at messing up yet again.
As we rock she strokes my hair,
tender, accepting, loving, forgiving.
Invisible cord twines around,
pulses through the two of us,
too green and strong for stupidity,
pigheadedness, or sins
for which I'm sorry to break.

VI

Roadside shoe no longer accuses.
Like weekend yard waste waiting curbside,
it's simply a pruned part of me.
Leave it there, God whispers.
A reminder of who you are:
Good enough mother
treasured daughter
fruit-bearer.

A Piece of Heaven on Earth

Look at the birds of the air: they neither sow nor reap nor gather into barns and yet your heavenly Father feeds them. Are you not of more value than they? And which of you by being anxious can add one cubit to his span of life?
—Matthew 6:26-27

Joel and I jump into the van on the first day of summer vacation and drive to Parky's Farm. Located five minutes from our house, Parky's is part of our county park system and has proved to be the perfect place for my can't-sit-still-for-a-single-minute son. It has also proved to be the perfect place for Joel's often overwhelmed mom.

We park the car and walk past the stables where Joel takes horseback lessons on Saturdays. Except for the crunch of our footsteps on gravel, everything is quiet.

I hold a finger to my lips. "The horses are sleeping. Listen. Can you hear them snoring?"

Joel laughs. I've never been known for my sense of humor, but in the eyes of my son I'm a comedian. Like his father, Wally, Joel has a talent for bringing out my silly side. As we walk past the barn, the mixed odors of manure and hay transport me back to my early teens when summer meant the sounds and smells of farm animals at the county fairgrounds, right across the street from our home on Randall Avenue.

Joel stops to talk to the big black and white cow in the paddock. "Hey cow! How ya doing?" The cow responds with a moo, ambling toward the fence. Joel reaches out and pats her on the nose. Talking to cows is one of our favorite family pastimes when we take rides in the country.

"Moo!" Joel yells. The cow backs off, not sure what to make of this fourteen-year-old guy whose voice is just starting to change.

We laugh and walk on toward the pond. Joel stops to pick up a handful of rocks and throws them in the water. A school of fish surfaces, expecting to find bread on the water. Disappointed, they dive back under the surface.

We head toward the little dock that stretches into the pond, Joel running ahead of me. "Don't feed the ducks," a sign warns. I sigh. So many rules. But we've brought stale bread for the fish, not the ducks, and Joel's attention is captivated for all of two minutes as he throws big chunks into the muddy water and watches the fish rise again, writhing and wide-mouthed, to gobble down their unexpected feast.

"Geese!" Joel cries, distracted from the fish as a flock of Canada geese lands with military precision in the field behind us. "Oh no," I moan. Joel will spend the next ten minutes chasing each and every goose into the pond, which is where, in his mind, they belong. There is no talking him out of this ritual. Believe me, I've tried on numerous occasions. Joel takes off running. By the time he is done he is flushed and breathless, proud of himself for having accomplished his goal. The geese swim, their feathers ruffled, their necks arched and haughty. I'm amazed, once again, that Joel has escaped the chase without being goosed. It is a minor miracle.

I plop down on the bench next to the pond and raise my face to the sun, closing my eyes in pleasure.

"Horse!" Joel says, pulling my arm.

"Go ahead," I answer. "I'm just going to sit here and enjoy the sun."

Joel looks at me quizzically. *Really?* I can see the question in his eyes.

"Go ahead. You're a big guy. I'll meet you over there in a few minutes."

Joel grins and walks the path around the pond, heading for the paddock where the ponies munch on long grass. He turns repeatedly to look at me, smiles, and waves. I wave back. I know how protective we have been—have had to be—and how a little bit of independence is just what Joel needs.

I soak in the sun and watch clouds scud across the wide-open sky. The fragrance of fresh-cut grass perfumes the air. In this moment, I am perfectly satisfied. No worries about the long summer ahead, historically a difficult time for Joel. No guilt about what I haven't done right over the past year. No place to go, nothing to do, no one to impress. I am simply here, in this place, watching my son walk tall in his newfound freedom; watching him hike across the hill on the other side of the pond, intent on feeding handfuls of grass to the ponies who wait patiently for his arrival.

Prayer

Lord, sometimes I think heaven will be a lot like Parky's Farm. Not just in the way it looks, smells, and sounds—long grass undulating in the wind under a big sky, the scent of fresh-mown hay, the sweet song of a red-winged blackbird carrying on the wind—but in the way it feels—a place of sanctuary, a place where I can be myself without needing to please anyone else, a place of gratitude, praise, and worship. Thank you for this son of mine, who in his neediness keeps bringing me back to this place. This place of refuge. This place that feels like a little piece of heaven on earth. Amen.

A New Song

Joel grabs the ukulele off the shelf and holds it out to Stacey, the college student who works with him three afternoons a week. "James Taylor," he commands, handing her the instrument.

"I don't know any James Taylor, Joel," Stacey says. "Let's make up a song."

Standing at the kitchen sink peeling potatoes for that night's dinner, I listen to the two of them talking and laughing in the family room. My mind drifts back to the day, one year earlier, when Stacey blew into our lives.

It was a blue-skied, breezy day in May. It didn't feel like spring. I was too exhausted to see the new life blossoming all around me, much less enjoy it.

At age fourteen, with hormones surging, Joel and his simmering anxiety were erupting more and more frequently in fits of aggression. We never knew when he might grab someone's hair, latching on so tight it took two people to pry his fingers loose. He pulled eyeglasses from people's faces, sometimes breaking the frames or lenses. When women or girls ventured too far into his personal space, he pulled their necklaces and earrings.

We were working with a doctor who specialized in autism, as well as a psychiatrist, play therapist, physical therapist, speech therapist, and occupational therapist. We had tried numerous medications and therapies, but nothing seemed to work. I lived in constant fear of the next explosion.

I finally called Joel's case worker at the county Board of Mental Retardation and said we needed more help in our home. He did the paperwork to fund more hours for respite. Finally, the agency we worked with called, saying they had a college student, majoring in music therapy, who was interested in meeting Joel. Her name was Stacey.

No way, I thought, the moment I met her. *No way this willowy young woman who can't weigh an ounce over 120 pounds can deal with my 180 pound son. She's not big enough to deal with his tantrums, his hair-pulling. Look at her long, wavy hair, for goodness sake! It's screaming, "Pull me! Pull me!"*

The tinny sound of the ukulele pulls me back into the present. My fingers are numb from holding the potatoes under cold, running water.

"Let's make up a song about the work you're doing at school, Joel." Stacey tunes the strings as she talks to my son. "What's that new job you're doing?"

Joel has recently started a work-study program where he travels into the community two afternoons a week to learn janitorial work. I shake my head. Stacey knows that Joel rarely answers direct questions.

"Trash," Joel says.

I turn off the water and set down the potato peeler, tiptoeing toward the family room door so I can hear more clearly.

"Do you like your job?" Stacey asks as she strums the ukulele.

Joel laughs.

"Joel likes to do the trash?" Stacey asks.

Joel laughs again.

"Okay. I think I've got a song here. Listen, and then you can sing it along with me, okay?"

Strumming two chords, Stacey begins to sing.

Joel likes to do the trash.
Joel likes to do the trash.
Joel likes to do the trash, with his . . .

Stacey stops singing, and waits for Joel to fill in the blank.

It takes Joel a few minutes to understand what she wants, but Stacey patiently sings the words over and over again, pausing at the end, waiting for Joel to insert a word of his choice. From the doorway I watch Joel's frown relax into a grin.

"Girlfriend!" he whispers.

Stacey laughs that contagious belly laugh that so drew me to her in the beginning. "There we go! Great lyrics!"

Joel likes to do the trash.
Joel likes to do the trash.
Joel likes to do the trash,
With his girlfriend.

She ends the song with a flamenco-like flourish. Joel giggles and then reaches out and touches the ukulele. "Joel likes to do the trash?" He wants her to sing it again. Stacey begins the song again. *Joel likes to do the trash . . .*

I stand in the doorway, watching the easy way Stacey interacts with my son. It hasn't been perfect, this relationship. But I have been amazed by this young woman's total trust in Joel.

Instead of flinching when he reaches out for her hair, Stacey usually manages to redirect his attention and his hands. When he does grab her long waves, she remains calm, gently pries his fingers loose, quietly tells him to use his words, and goes on to the next activity.

This young woman, who spends three afternoons a week in our home, is intelligent, idealistic, enthusiastic, and creative. Her smile, which eats up half of her face and continues to her eyes, is contagious.

Clad in jeans, a t-shirt, and sandals, Stacey reminds me of myself in my college days. How fresh and new and hopeful the world had looked then. The day I interviewed Stacey, I felt old and grumpy and short on hope. I hired her, despite her inexperience, her long hair, and her willowy size, hoping that maybe, just maybe, some of her enthusiasm would rub off on me. I knew that negative attitudes were just as contagious as smiles and laughter. Joel needed a mom who smiled more.

I walk through the family room door, drying my hands on a dish towel. "I love that song, Joel! Can I sing along?" Fifteen minutes later I'm laughing so hard that tears stream down my face.

Prayer

Thank you, Lord, for the people you send into our lives on the wind of your Spirit. I thank you for Stacey, who not only ministers to my son through the gift of music and unconditional love, but who mirrors my best self back to me, who helps me excavate that hope-filled place in my heart that is buried under the mud of exhaustion and the demands of day-to-day care giving. Bless her, Lord, for blessing us. Amen.

Trash Man for Heaven

I do not cease to give thanks for you, remembering you in my prayers, that the God of our Lord Jesus Christ, the Father of glory, may give you a spirit of wisdom and of revelation in the knowledge of him, having the eyes of your hearts enlightened, that you may know what is the hope to which he has called you.
—Ephesians 1:16-18

"Who will be the sweeper while you're gone?"

When I announced that I was flying to Wisconsin to visit my grandparents for a weekend, my son Matt's plaintive question, asked with three-year-old sincerity, sent my already bedraggled self-esteem into a tailspin. I dropped the broom where I stood, leaving a pile of lunch crumbs and wilted grass in the middle of the kitchen floor.

It was the late 1970s, the decade of women's lib and shattered glass ceilings. Okay, so I chose to be a stay-at-home mom. So I traded paychecks and power for spilt milk, sticky hugs, and a daily barrage of unanswerable questions. So I spent an inordinate amount of time sweeping my newly refinished hardwood floors.

Who will be the sweeper while you're gone?

The entire essence of me suddenly compressed itself into what could be swept into a dustpan and thrown away.

Who will be the sweeper while you're gone?

Fast forward twenty-five years. Incredibly, that question still echoes as I attempt to make peace with the job for which Joel is being trained—trash collection.

Joel's behavior difficulties at school have improved significantly since he began a work-study program that enables him to leave school after lunch each day to work in the community.

Trash collection is the perfect job for Joel, really. It enables him to be constantly on the move. For someone who finds it impossible to sit still, this job spells freedom. It is concrete, with a visible beginning and end. It requires a minimal use of fine motor skills. It also stretches Joel by requiring attention to the task as he moves from room to room, something he finds difficult but a skill he will need for many life situations.

Considering the job is so well suited to Joel's unique personality and capabilities, why do I find myself cringing when friends ask me what Joel is learning at school? Why do I keep searching for a more "dignified" expression for trash collection?

Trash. Think of the synonyms. Garbage. Junk. Rubbish. That's a lot of baggage for a five-letter word.

Saddled with several medical and mental health diagnoses, my son already carries enough of the world's baggage. Do I really want him trained as a *trash collector?*

Four words, heard in the stillness of meditation, shed new light on that very question.

Trash man for heaven.

I shake my head as if to clear it. The words sound again in the silence.

Trash man for heaven.

My attention riveted, I wait for more.

Joel is doing his job—he's collecting the trash. He's good at this job. It's an important job. Joel is humble. He's obedient. He desires above all else to please those he loves. And so he does his job—a job you see as somehow below you—without complaint. The Kingdom is a more beautiful place because of Joel.

My mind's eye moves to the neighborhoods around our city where debris litters the streets—fast-food wrappers, soggy newspapers, advertising circulars in plastic bags. I see Joel and his Starfire Club buddies donning gloves and walking the streets, picking up trash, knowing they'll get an ice-cream when finished, proud of their efforts to make the neighborhood a better place.

I think of all those wastebaskets at church where Joel volunteers, the ones he empties three days a week. I see them overflow with crumpled paper, used tissues, discolored apple cores, and smelly banana peels on the days he doesn't work.

The Spirit's words reverberate through my mind.

He does his job—a job you see as somehow below you.

I think again of all those synonyms for trash. Garbage. Junk. Rubbish. This time, a veil lifts and I see them in a new light—they are the logs in my eyes which I refuse to acknowledge. They represent my worldly tendency to classify, categorize, and ultimately judge.

Joel is humble. He's obedient. He desires above all else to please those he loves.

I think of the upside-down nature of God's kingdom and of how Joel, in his poverty, models Christ's way of obedience and simplicity and unconditional love.

Trash man for heaven.

I suddenly hear it for what it is. A nickname. A term of endearment for a deeply loved and cherished son.

On the heels of that thought Matt's long-ago question echoes through my mind.

Who will be the sweeper while you're gone?

The words lose their sting as I realize, on a heart level, that God loves me as well, not for what I do or accomplish, but simply for who I am.

Prayer

Dear Lord, forgive me for gazing upon my son and his job with worldly eyes. Help me to see with the eyes of my heart, Lord. Help me to see Joel as you see Joel—perfect in your sight. And help me to see myself as you see me, Lord—precious and beloved. Amen.

Pearl beyond Price

Blonde-haired
blue-eyed
Joel smiles shyly from jeweled frame
Spirit glows
illuminating
rubies, emeralds, amethysts
glittering 'round his face

Pearl most precious
beyond any price
peace
order
comfort
serenity
shattered, all
by disability

Cognitive impairments
demanding, always
undivided attention
patience
watchfulness
creativity
beyond, at times,
the humanly possible

And yet . . .

Bringer of light
Joel illuminates
darkness of selfishness
Bearer of wisdom
he enlightens
eyes of hearts with understanding
Giver of grace
he brightens even
darkest days with unexpected joy

Blonde-haired
blue-eyed
Joel's half-smile
illuminates jeweled frame
Spirit glows
gift of God
pearl beyond price

Walking the Labyrinth

*Thou dost show me the path of life; in thy presence there is
fullness of joy, in thy right hand are pleasures for evermore.*
—*Psalm 16:11*

"Why don't you bring your son with you? We would love to
meet him, and there are plenty of children's activities here at
the ranch. We'll find a big buddy to hang out with him."

Joel is welcome—*welcome!* It has been so long since Joel
has been invited anywhere.

I've been asked to lead a retreat for parents and grandparents of children with disabilities at Ghost Ranch Conference
Center. I fly to New Mexico with Wally and Joel. I carry my
heart in my hand, hoping against hope that somehow *this*
will be the place where Joel will break out of his pattern of
anxiety-induced aggression.

Wrong.

I return from an intense morning session where we've been
exploring the stages of grief experienced by parents when
a child is born with a disability or becomes disabled later
in life through illness or accident. Wally, who had left the
workshop early to check on Joel, greets me at the cabin door.
Yet another report of hair-pulling. Even with a big buddy
accompanying him to activities, Joel is acting out. *Will it
never end? He's sixteen, for heaven's sake! Are we going to*

deal with this for the rest of our lives? How am I supposed to do my job when I'm worrying about Joel hurting other children? I'm so tired!

Frustration. Anger. Impatience. Powerlessness. A churning stew of emotions, quickly reaching the boiling point, forces me out of the cabin. The screen door slams with a satisfying crash. I walk, half-trot, head down, avoiding eye contact with fellow retreatants, until I realize I'm lost.

"Excuse me! Do you know where the labyrinth is?" My voice, to my surprise, sounds abrasive and rude.

The woman points, says something about wind chimes. I walk between buildings, the sound of satisfied voices in the art center grating on my nerves.

Melodic wind chimes. A carefully placed pile of smooth stones. A feather blowing in the breeze. An oasis of calm in a challenging week. No wonder I'd walked right by, oblivious.

For the first time since arriving at the ranch, I am alone. The labyrinth lies before me, a large circle, its outer rim delineated by bricks, buried narrow edge up; its inner paths consist of soft-ball-sized rocks, some round and smooth, others jagged and asymmetrical. The path in the circle is clearly marked. Nerve ends jangling, I remember the brochure's assurance that the labyrinth is not a maze; as an aid to prayer, the path to the circle's center is easily followed.

I take a deep breath, blow it out. Breathe deeply again, willing tension away. Wiggle shoulders, shake hands, close eyes for a moment.

I step onto the path. To my surprise, it leads directly to the center-most ring.

"This can't be right!" My voice sounds foreign, irate. I turn and walk back the way I had come, until I'm standing outside the circle, looking in, willing a clearer perspective.

The entrance path definitely leads to the center, then wanders back to a circle mid-way between the inner and outer rings.

Deciding to forge my own path, I step over rocks into the outer ring and begin to walk, counter clock-wise. I run into a dead-end and have to turn back. By now my agitation is boiling in great rolling bubbles. My breath comes in gasps. Again, I close my eyes and inhale deeply, blow it out, breathe deeply again.

The path is clearly marked. Put one foot in front of the other and trust. The words rise up, unbidden, through seething emotions.

"I can do that," I hear myself answer.

And so I begin. I step onto the path so clearly laid out. Walk slowly, deliberately. One foot in front of the other. To the center. Away from the center. One foot in front of the other. Trust. Left, right, forward, backward, I weave my way around the circle, the path I'm walking making no sense. Just when I think I've made my way to journey's end, I find myself back near where I began.

The words come as a mantra with my breath. "Put one foot in front of the other and trust."

Wind chime harmonies drift on the breeze. A blur of bluebird flashes through my peripheral vision. A mutter of thunder threatens as light rain begins to fall, releasing metallic scent from desert sand, dirt, and rocks. Still, I walk forward, one foot in front of the other.

Path opens, without warning, onto circle's center. Several boulders invite rest and meditation. I sit. Skies open. Palms up, I greet the rain. Contemplating mementos left by previous wayfarers, I realize I have nothing to leave but my frustration, anger, and fear of the future.

I lay them down and walk, head up, to greet the self I left behind the screen door's slam.

Prayer

Teach me, Lord, to walk forward on a daily basis in faith, to put one foot in front of the other, trusting in your goodness, your mercy, your faithfulness, trusting in your plan for my life, for Joel's life, for the life of our family. Amen.

Of Walnut Trees and Angels

So we do not lose heart. Though our outer nature is wasting away, our inner nature is being renewed every day. For this slight momentary affliction is preparing for us an eternal weight of glory beyond all comparison, because we look not to the things that are seen but to the things that are unseen; for the things that are seen are transient, but the things that are unseen are eternal.
—2 Corinthians 4:16-18

It is Wednesday, August 29, and the walnut tree has already begun her letting go. Yellow leaves spiral gently to the ground. Joel stands at the kitchen window, transfixed.

"The trees are falling," he whispers, his voice wonder-filled.

Fall is Joel's favorite season. He can stand for great blocks of time—this fifteen-year-old with virtually no attention span—and be transported into some other realm of existence as the trees go about their business of letting go.

I set the laundry basket on the table and join him. The lazy, swirling movement of the leaves is mesmerizing.

"Yes, the trees are falling," I agree absentmindedly, for once not correcting his word choice.

I stand as if in a dream, my mind far away. I have been finding it more and more difficult to live in the present moment, my brain forever whizzing into the future. *What if Joel's school year is a repeat of last year's disaster? What if the new meds don't work? What if his aggression gets worse? What if I can't handle the stress any longer? Where will he live as an adult? How will we handle letting him go out into the world, this child we've tended so carefully—this child*

*who has cost us so much in energy and patience—this child
who has gifted us so freely with love?*

Watching the golden wings of walnut leaves helicopter to the ground, I am suddenly filled with a dread of the dark, dank days of winter to come. Picking up the laundry basket, I pull myself away from the view as well as from the thought.

I put the clothes away and come back to the kitchen, only to find that Joel has left his window watch. I call his name.

"Basement," he answers, his voice floating, deep and man-like, up the stairwell. To my surprise, he sounds just like his father. While I've been busy worrying, he's been growing up. Although cognitively he has yet to pass the age of four, at fifteen the hormones are right on schedule.

I peer down the steps into semidarkness.

"What are you doing down there?"

Uncharacteristically, he answers immediately.

"Lookin' for angels." He steps into the light at the bottom of the stairs and looks up at me, his face earnest. "The trees are falling," he continues, as if that explains it all.

"I know the leaves are falling, Joel. Fall comes before winter. Christmas comes in winter, honey."

"Time to get the angels out," he insists, pointing to the cupboard where we keep the Christmas decorations. "The trees are falling!"

Joel's logic defies me until a sermon I heard years ago by Tony Campolo pops into my head. Time as we know it, Campolo reminded me, does not exist for God. Past, present, and future exist at the same time in God's mind. There is no past, no present, no future. Simply the sacred *now*.

In God's time, as the walnut drops her leaves on this hot and humid August afternoon, it is, simultaneously, that very first Christmas. Even as angels announce that holy event, Joel announces to me, on this Wednesday afternoon at the tail end of summer in the year 2000, that something sacred is happening right this very moment. Through the walnut tree, through Joel, through angels stored in the basement, I am being called to live *now*—today—not in the unknown and uncontrollable future, not in the past with its guilts and regrets—but in the present, holy moment.

I walk back to the kitchen window and allow myself to be mesmerized by the beautiful sight in front of me, to truly experience walnut leaves fluttering to the ground. The background noise of all my anxieties, as well as the sound of Joel rustling through the basement cupboard, is drowned out by the sigh of a late summer breeze and echoes of angel song.

Prayer

O Lord, no intelligence testing, no behavior graphs, no diagnosis will ever sum up my son's capabilities. He teaches me daily about the eternal nature of your kingdom, if I stop long enough to listen. Today he gave me a glimpse of the weight of your glory. How does the world catalog that kind of spiritual insight? Help me be open to all he has to teach me: how to let go of anxiety about the future, of guilt and shame over the past, and how to simply live in the present moment—here, now, today. Amen.

Emmaus Eyes

And their eyes were opened and they recognized him; and he vanished out of their sight. They said to each other, "Did not our hearts burn within us while he talked to us on the road, while he opened to us the scriptures?"
—Luke 24:31-32

Finished with our game
of funny faces
Joel cups my face
between his palms

An offering of praise

Thirteen going on three
his childlike eyes
arrest my gaze
burn with new intelligence

Search me
Know me
Forgive me
Love me

Remembered words drop
like pebbles
in the pond of our play

The foolish
shall shame the wise

Funny chipmunk face
his favorite
startles meditation
My heart ignites

Resurrection

Behold, if any one is in Christ, he is a new creation;
the old has passed away, behold, the new has come.
—2 Corinthians 5:17

Easter Sunday, Apalachicola, Florida.

There's not enough room for everyone to gather around the dining room table, so Wally's sister Anne seats Wally, Joel, and me at the table with Gus and Evelyn, a couple we've just met. Anne joins the rest of her guests on the screened-in porch overlooking the bayside park, where the water shimmers in the distance. I would rather be sitting on the porch where a nice breeze is blowing than stuck inside at a table with strangers, but Anne knows Joel doesn't have the fine-motor control to eat with a plate on his lap—he needs to sit at a table.

Resentment bubbles up, along with a big dose of self-pity. It had been just Wally, Joel, and me worshipping on the beach this morning. I miss the group of friends who used to meet us here and our beachside Easter celebrations with guitar, Scripture, and impromptu sermons. And I miss our sons Matt and Justin, who no longer join us for this yearly Florida trek.

God may be unchangeable, I grouse as I help Anne carry food from kitchen to the buffet table, *but life itself is nothing but change.* The sky is blue and dotted with cumulus clouds, and a balmy breeze makes the palmettos clatter. Magpies raise a ruckus in the top of the live oak tree in the front yard. Despite my sour mood, I smile and try to make small talk as we dig into Easter dinner—country ham, pan-fried grouper, potato salad, baked beans, and a green salad. The last time we celebrated Easter together here, Wally's dad and Anne soaked a country ham for days, and even after all the soaking it took a saw to cut it. I can still hear the sound of Dad's laughter that day, even though he's been gone for five years now. Tears prickle behind my eyelids.

Wally, Gus, and Evelyn are having no trouble keeping a conversation going. A big man, the planes of Gus's weathered, brown face speak of Native ancestry. He's a contractor and has been rebuilding Anne's back porch. I listen with half an ear to talk of Apalachicola's building boom, astronomical property values, and Gus's work projects.

Joel sits between me and Wally. I give up on the small talk and busy myself by cutting his ham into bite-size pieces, reminding him with hand gestures to wipe his face. At fifteen, he is still a messy eater. Years of work both at home and school have not made a dent in his propensity to cram as much food as possible, as quickly as possible, into his mouth. Sometimes it's embarrassing, especially when eating out or when, like today, we share a meal with strangers.

Suddenly I am aware that Gus is watching Joel, a curious expression on his face. A flush starts in my chest and moves upwards. *Why is he staring? Can't he tell that Joel is disabled?*

As usual, Joel finishes his meal before the rest of us have barely tucked into plates piled high. I excuse myself to help him find his tape player and headset and get him situated in the living room. If I'm lucky, I'll have ten minutes to finish my meal before being dragged outside. *Some Easter,* I think. Once again, I'm blinking back tears.

As I pull my chair back up to the table, Gus leans toward me and looks me in the eye.

"I can't help but notice your son is disabled. Do you mind telling me what his disability is?"

My mind says, *Oh, please.* My mouth forms words, but I'm unable to conjure a smile to accompany them.

"For years we had a diagnosis of moderate mental retardation," I answer. "But a couple of years ago Joel was diagnosed with autism as well."

Gus and Evelyn listen, nodding their heads, and asking a few more questions. Gus leans even closer to me, his gaze commanding. I can't turn away.

"In my culture, which is Lakota Sioux, your son would be considered a gift from God."

Goosebumps prickle up and down my arms. His steady eyes still hold mine.

"Lakota Sioux believe that children like yours are sent from heaven to teach us compassion. They are treated with the greatest respect, regardless of their diagnosis or behavior."

The four of us have fallen quiet for a moment. Through the dining room archway we see Joel sitting on the couch, engrossed in a Wee Sing tape.

At that moment, Anne sweeps into the dining room, announcing that dessert is served. Chairs shuffle, plates clatter, laughter replaces quiet conversation, and Easter dawns in my heart.

Prayer

Lord, I praise you that we are resurrected from our self-made tombs on a daily basis, if we only open our eyes and ears to the soundings of your Spirit. Thank you for this "chance" Easter seating at a table with strangers, so that your truth might break through my world-weary heart. Keep reminding me that while your love is never-changing, life in your kingdom is about constant regeneration and renewal. Help me embrace that kind of change. Let me allow you to reclaim and reshape me daily with the truth of your love. A love that is unconditional and compassionate—a no-strings-attached kind of love—the kind of love Joel continually teaches me to embrace. Amen.

Desert Baptism

Behold, I am doing a new thing; now it springs forth, do you not perceive it? I will make a way in the wilderness and rivers in the desert.
—Isaiah 43:19

A mountain of sheer granite looms behind me and my friends, Patti and Alice. Ahead, the trail winds through rock outcroppings, sparse vegetation, and an occasional and surprisingly beautiful stand of wildflowers. I've been plucked from the desert of day-to-day care-giving and placed here in Palm Desert, California, through an unexpected, last-minute invitation.

The three of us hike for three miles, stopping often to uncap our water bottles, drinking in great draughts. The trail climbs upward, gaining altitude, and the barren brownness stretches out in all directions. The sky is a blue bowl, pressing down, and a dry wind sucks the moisture out of everything it touches. Out of shape, I gasp for breath as I put one foot in front of the other, pushing upward.

We've been hiking for nearly two hours when the oasis appears below us, stretched out like a green goliath in the shimmering desert sun. As we approach it comes into focus as a very real, lush and verdant valley. Scrambling down the rock-strewn trail, we see that the valley, lined with hundreds of palm trees, is cut through and fed by a sparkling stream.

Desiring some time alone I dawdle behind my friends, sit on the edge of the stream, and take off my hiking boots and socks. I submerge my hot, tired feet in the water, which is translucent green and surprisingly cold. Palm leaves clatter overhead, and the sound of a turtledove carries on the breeze.

Several months earlier, the Spirit had instructed me in prayer to withdraw from as much activity as possible and to spend time simply resting in God's presence. I had been slow to listen and obey. The fruits of that disobedience were depression and exhaustion. God had wanted good things for me, but I had been too prideful to respond to my Creator's loving guidance. I had been intent on being super-mom to six-teen-year-old Joel, super-wife, super-friend, super-Christian. Superwoman had finally made a crash landing.

Desperate for help, I had sought prayer from Cheryl, a friend with a heart for healing ministry. Wally and Cheryl's husband, Jim, had joined us.

Cheryl anointed my forehead with oil, and the warmth of three pairs of hands began to melt away some of my resistance. As they prayed a vision arose. I saw myself climbing a mountainside, the steep and rocky path in front of me obscured by thick, gray fog. My heart began to beat wildly. I forced myself to breathe deeply.

"What do you see, Kathy?" Cheryl's voice broke through my panic.

I described the rock-strewn path, the steep incline, the fog.

"What else do you see?" she asked.

I looked around but couldn't see a thing for the fog.

"Nothing," I answered. "I see nothing." Again, my pulse quickened.

Suddenly, in the vision, I felt a pressure on my left elbow. A hand, a strong and capable hand, gripped my arm, steadied me, guided me.

I leaned into my unseen companion and walked, with his strength, more confidently up the path. My anxiety receded, replaced by a spirit of boldness. It was if I had just received a blood transfusion.

Upward we climbed, up and up and up, until we reached the mountain's summit, our heads finally clearing the clouds. I looked down at a mountain shrouded in fog and then up at a clear blue sky.

I caught just a glimpse of my companion, the one whose strong right arm had supported me up the treacherous path.

"Thank you, Lord," I whispered.

Later that evening the invitation to California had arrived via e-mail. My friend Patti had just emerged from a battle with breast cancer, and as a celebratory gift her brother had given her a week at his condo in Palm Desert. She and another friend, Alice, had made plans weeks before for a golf vacation.

"Kathy, I know this is very last minute, but I've had the strongest feeling all week that you're supposed to go on this trip with us," the e-mail had read. "We're leaving in two days. We'd love for you to join us if you can. I know you don't golf, but you could probably use the rest, and there's a nice pool there . . ."

Never had I found it so easy to get away for a week. The arrangements came together effortlessly: calendar cleared, inexpensive airline tickets purchased, after-school care for Joel lined up, summer clothes washed and packed.

And here I sit, at rest in a true-life desert oasis, bare feet soaking in a stream in the midst of a harsh and unforgiving land.

My feet and my spirit, both so tired from the journey, rest in refreshing waters. Bending down, I cup my hands and splash cool water on my sunburned cheeks and forehead. Somewhere deep inside me a shift has taken place.

Lifting my face to the sky, I watch sunlight dance in the cottonwood trees, listen to the throaty calls of two turtledoves, and breathe in the scent of new life.

I close my eyes and let myself experience the Kingdom come. Thinking back to the prayer session with Cheryl, Wally, and Jim, I remember the unseen companion who had accompanied me up that foggy mountainside. I imagine him sitting beside me, bare feet submerged in the cold, clear water.

My shriveled soul expands. Just as I think I will burst with joy, Jesus splashes me with a quick movement of his foot through the water; baptizes me with his laughter.

Prayer

Lord, how can I thank you for this marvelous gift? I will never look at my desert experiences in quite the same way again. When the road is rocky, the landscape bare, and thirst my constant companion, I will remember this very real oasis. But more importantly, I will remember your presence beside me at the stream, and I will remember the sound of your laughter. Amen.

Desert Walk

They walk, sandaled
mother, father, son
(two sons grown, flown,
this one called disabled)
ground shifting,
pebbles branding tender in-steps

Boy's voice, too big in town, drifts
through shimmering vastness,
dwarfed
"It's a good day for snakes!"
Poking juniper with a stick
he releases incense
and memories of worship
but here there is only
confession and thirst

Ahead the earth buckles
heaves, path winding
upward through jutting
rocks born of heat
and pressure, sculpted
stones; henna, russet
salmon, flame

Weary feet seek footholds
up and over fallen boulders
walls narrow, form passageway
wide enough for one

"Water," whispers the boy
Resting, single-file
silenced by wind-song
they drink together
mother, father, son
in the shadow
of the Rock

Lessons from the Pew

Praise the LORD! Praise God in his sanctuary, praise him in his mighty firmament! Praise him with timbrel and dance! Praise him with strings and pipe! Praise him with sounding cymbals; praise him with loud clashing cymbals!
—Psalm 150:1, 4-5

Lately I've been asking myself why Wally and I are so pig-headedly determined to mold Joel into a proper Presbyterian. A Presbyterian who does what all good Presbyterians do—sit when told to sit, stand when told to stand, pray when told to pray, sing when told to sing, and above all, sit quietly in between the standing and singing and praying.

Like trying to fit a square peg into a round hole, it's an exercise in futility and frustration.

Typically, Sunday morning looks something like this:

Joel enters into worship wholeheartedly. Or maybe I should say whole-bodily. He bounces to the beat of the drums, claps his hands, thrusts his arms heavenward, and stomps his feet.

The first inkling of trouble begins during "prayers for the people." These prayers set Joel to thinking, and, unfortunately, Joel almost always thinks out loud.

"Someone died. Oh no. It's sad when people die. Sometimes people die. My papa died. I miss my papa."

During the Scripture reading, the ants in Joel's pants begin to divide and multiply. (Think of the Egyptian plagues.) Words spoken solemnly from the pulpit mean little to Joel, so he kicks his feet under the pew in front of us. Soon bored with this, he leans over and sniffs Wally's leather jacket or wipes his nose on the sleeve of my blouse.

During the pastoral prayer he decides it is way too quiet and begins knocking on the wooden pew.

"Who's there?" he giggles. "Who's there?"

With the knocking game brought to a halt by whichever parent is sitting next to the offending hand, Joel turns to stare at the people behind us. On days when he's really antsy, he reaches out his hand and lets it hover just inches from the head of the person sitting in front of him.

If he *really* wants to leave this intolerable, sit-still-and-be-quiet place, he pulls out the "I'm starving" ploy, delivered loud enough for the entire congregation to hear.

"Church over. I'm starving. Time for lunch. Amen!"

On a recent Communion Sunday, the elders lined up at the rear of the church and solemnly carried the elements up the aisle. There was Joel, energy fizzing over like a shook-up can of soda, our entire pew quaking with the frustrated movements of his sixteen-year-old, 190-pound frame. His chanted litany shattered the silence.

"Church is over! Church is over! Church is over! Amen!"

By the time church was over that Sunday, my head was pounding to the beat of the pulse in my ears. My litany, unlike Joel's, chanted under my breath *(this just isn't worth it, this just isn't worth it, this just isn't worth it),* did little to calm my jangled nerves.

Back to the square peg and round hole analogy. There are those of us who insist this feat can be accomplished. We're convinced that, if we just work hard enough, long enough, and smart enough, we can make that square peg slide in and out of its little round hole. We spend weeks (months, years) trying before we finally give up in sheer frustration. Or we whittle away at the edges of the peg with words, gestures, and attitudes until it finally, begrudgingly, slips into the hole, no longer recognizable as the peg it once was. Sometimes we even break the peg in the trying.

Why, I have to ask, are we willing to deface or break a peg before we think of finding a board with square holes?

On Sunday evening of the aforementioned Communion service, I reluctantly accompanied Wally and Joel to a community celebration commemorating Dr. Martin Luther King Jr., held at an African American church just down the street from our church. My reluctance stemmed not from the theme of the service nor its location, but from sheer panic at the thought of sitting through yet another church service with Joel.

The evening began with hand-clapping, foot-stomping worship and praise. Joel looked around, surprised and absolutly delighted to see that he wasn't the only whole-body worshipper present.

During the sermon, shouted words of encouragement punctuated the air. During the pastoral prayer a low muttering filled the worship space as many people prayed their own prayers out loud.

The proverbial light bulb illuminated my mind. We were sitting in a peg board full of square holes, and Joel slid into place as neatly as you please. There is nothing wrong with the way Joel worships. He worships with his heart, soul, *and* body. Asking him to sit still and be quiet for an hour is like asking a blind man to describe the new altar cloth or a deaf woman to take notes on the spoken sermon.

On the ride home that night I reached over and touched Wally's shoulder.

"It's like Joel *belonged* there tonight!"

So, what do we do? Do we leave a church we love? Leave friends we hold dear? Do we encourage our church to loosen up and learn from Joel about how to integrate worship into the body? Do we shift our perspective on our son's differences from embarrassment to acceptance, letting him worship (and interrupt) however he chooses?

The answer to that is not yet clear. But this I know beyond a shadow of a doubt: Square pegs were never meant to fit into round holes. It's time to break the mold.

Prayer

Dear Lord, you tell us the greatest commandment is to love the Lord with all our soul, heart, and mind. Joel's love for you is a fragrant offering. Help me, as well as our church family, realize that wonderful aroma wafting through the air comes from our pew—the pew that is quaking and shaking. Amen.

Joel's Got a Girlfriend

Behold, you are beautiful, my beloved, truly lovely.
—Song of Solomon 1:16

We're in the car, running errands. I'm driving, and Joel is in the backseat, passenger side. Stopping for a red light, my mind wanders, only to be jolted back to reality by a loud smacking sound coming from the backseat. Turning my head to investigate, my eye is caught by five feminine faces in the car next to us. My first impression is that these cute teenage girls are laughing, waving, and blowing kisses at me. My head continues its swivel toward the backseat. My eyes light upon Joel who is smacking his hand and throwing, in an extravagant gesture, a kiss out the car window. The light turns green and I accelerate. Joel begins to sing an old schoolyard ditty.

Joel's got a girlfriend, Joel's got a girlfriend, Joel's got a girlfriend.

We're at the neighborhood shopping center. Coming out of the store, we round the corner to the library. A teenage girl with spiked red hair is standing in the shadows of the building, talking on a cell phone. I walk a good fifteen yards before I realize Joel is no longer beside me. I turn around to see him, stopped dead in his tracks, a couple of yards away from the girl. Again, he's smacking his hand with gusto and throwing kisses with the concentration of a major league pitcher. The girl's face is as red as her hair. I run back, grab Joel's hand, and pull him toward the library, repeating my new mantra: "Joel, that's not appropriate. Use your words if you want to say hi to someone." I hear him singing under his breath.

Joel's got a girlfriend. Joel's got a girlfriend. Joel's got a girlfriend.

Wait a minute. What's this wistful feeling rising up inside of me? My boy is, after all, seventeen years old. His hormonal development, if nothing else, is right on track. It's somehow comforting to know that something is developing properly. Am I absolutely irrational to feel this way?

Go ahead. Call me an incurable romantic. Call me hopelessly naïve. Call me just plain stupid if you want. But I can't let go of this belief that everyone deserves a chance at romance.

I'm talking about that fluttery feeling in the stomach when a certain guy or girl walks into the room; that indescribable electrical charge that jumps from fingertip to fingertip as that certain someone grabs your hand; the sensation of melting as you snuggle together on the couch; the fireworks that fill your field of vision when you close your eyes to kiss.

A few years ago my middle son, Justin, and I watched a television special entitled "Sex with Cindy Crawford." The intent of the documentary (much tamer than the racy title implied) was to foster discussion between parents and teens around the topic of sexuality.

"Mom, what are we going to do about Joel's sex life when he's all grown up?" Justin had asked.

Ouch! Not knowing what to say, I asked Justin what he thought.

It turned out Justin hadn't really thought about it up until that very moment, but he had suddenly realized his little brother was going to have sexual feelings just like the rest of humanity, and just what were we (meaning his dad and me, who should always know the answers to these things) going to do about it.

I've spent a lot of time since then thinking about that question, without coming up with a lot of answers. I've found, in the meantime, that when I mention Joel's new penchant for throwing kisses at girls, I am sometimes met with embarrassment and an uncomfortable silence. It's as if I've stumbled onto taboo territory. Sexuality and the disabled? Oh no! Can't go there!

And yet, people who have disabilities have sexual feelings just like the rest of us. The child psychiatrist in charge of Joel's medications told us, not too long ago, that some of what we're seeing in Joel's aggressive behaviors might be a manifestation of his inability to understand what's going on in his body.

I remember back to when I was thirteen. Budding breasts, monthly menses, and an alternating sense of power and terror, excitement and embarrassment. My relationship with my father changed, it seemed, overnight. He no longer cuddled me on his lap, or even hugged me much. My body felt strange, foreign, as if it belonged to someone else. There were days I hated this strange new me, when I wanted nothing more than to go back to who I had been before. There were days I didn't want to get out of bed and days I felt like I could fly, days I hated my parents and days I cried because I loved them so much.

Again, I look at Joel, this little boy in a teenager's body, the man struggling to emerge. The mom in me wants to pull him back, wrap him in blue baby bunting, keep him swaddled and safe. I keep coming back to Justin's question. "What will we do about Joel's sex life when he's all grown up, Mom?"

The all-grown-up part is almost here.

Joel's got a girlfriend. Joel's got a girlfriend. Joel's got a girlfriend.

Call me an incurable romantic. Call me hopelessly naïve. Call me just plain stupid if you want. But I still think everyone deserves a chance at romance.

Prayer

Dear Lord, is it too much to expect that one day Joel will have a girlfriend? Is this another dream I have to give up for my son? This, along with the driver's license and the ability to vote, to father a child, to live totally on his own, to sell cranes with his father? So many dreams, unrealized. I admit my powerlessness in this situation, Lord, and ask your wisdom and guidance. Let my son live a full life, whatever that may look like. And let him know, dear Lord, that he is beautiful. Amen.

Life on the Edge

Ask, and it will be given you; seek, and you will find; knock, and it will be opened to you. For every one who asks receives, and he who seeks finds, and to him who knocks it will be opened.
—*Matthew 7:7-8*

Why? I groan as the bright June sun slips over the window sill, waking me from a dream. *Why didn't I sign Joel up for camp on Mondays?*

The day stretches out in front of us, seemingly endless. Embodied memories of Joel's early childhood—48-hour days—still have the power to elicit feelings of panic at the beginning of an unplanned day. Snow days, teacher conference days, summer days—any days that find me home alone with Joel (who is now seventeen) are almost certain to bring up what has long since become a conditioned response:

Help!

I call my friend Jen, a fellow nature-lover.

"I'm thinking about taking Joel to the Nature Center today. Want to come along?"

She does. I pack sandwiches, pretzels, and juice boxes. When Joel begins obsessing on the way to Jen's house, I know, with a mother's sixth sense, that it is going to be a difficult day.

"Where we going?"

"The Nature Center. We'll go for a hike."

"Where is it?"

"Out in the country. It will take us half an hour to get there."

"Where is it?" he asks again. And again. And again. And again.

By the time we reach Jen's house, a mere ten-minute drive, I am ready to tear my hair out.

As usual, distraction proves a blessing as Jen hops into the van, buckles her seatbelt, and turns around to greet Joel.

"Hey, buddy! Great to see you!" Her enthusiasm cuts the tension, and Joel starts singing along to a Wee Sing tape I've shoved into the cassette player.

It is one of those perfect June days—the kind that brides pray for. Cottony clouds cast fast-moving shadows on the road in front of us. The world gleams so green you would swear you can hear the leaves and trees and grass growing.

Jen and I chat, catching up on what has happened since we last met. My anxiety vanishes in the wake of the wind pouring in through the van's open windows.

Fifteen minutes away from our destination Joel starts chanting a new mantra.

"I'm starving. I'm starving. I'm starving."

By the time I whip the van into a parking place at the Nature Center, my head is throbbing to the beat.

"I'm starving. I'm starving. I'm starving."

We quickly find a picnic spot next to a pond. Joel's sandwich is gone in two minutes flat. A new litany erupts.

"More! More! More! More!"

I look at Jen and whisper, "I have a feeling this is going to be a quick trip."

My body feels electrified—a mass of exposed nerve endings. Behaviors I had long been able to ignore, screen out, deal with halfway gracefully, now send me into a state of anxiety bordering on panic.

Jen reads the message beneath my words.

"Hey, Joel! Look at all the turtles on that log! Let's see how close we can get!"

In the van we had talked about all the animals and insects we might see at the Nature Center. Joel loves wildlife, and we've spent many a happy hour searching the woods behind our house for turtles and snakes. As we had approached the Nature Center, he had settled on the idea of finding a turtle.

Six turtles line up on a log in the pond, picture perfect. Joel takes a quick look before turning his back.

"No turtles. Snake. Find a snake," he says, picking up a stick and poking it into the grass along the path.

"Oh Joel, snakes are hard to see. I don't know if we'll find a snake today. Look, there's another turtle—a big one," Jen says.

"Snake!" Joel shouts. "Find a snake!"

"He's about to disintegrate," I tell Jen. "Let's go into the museum and find a mounted snake for him to look at, and then we'll leave."

We head inside. Ducks. Hawks. Geese. Fox. Everything under the sun except, wouldn't you know it, a snake.

I anticipate a difficult ride home. Perseveration. Agitation. Escalating anxiety. Next stop, temper tantrum. Under these circumstances, simply getting Joel to the van could be a major undertaking.

Motioning to Jen I shepherd Joel out the back door of the museum, hoping to avoid any crowds. The parking lot is a short walk away, past several bird feeders perched on poles planted in a patch of grass.

"Snake!" Joel yells.

"No snakes today, Joel. Time to go home," I say in my calmest I'm-not-going-to-lose-it voice.

"Oh my gosh," Jen breathes in a stage whisper.

Coiled up just yards in front of us, awaiting his lunch beneath a birdfeeder, is the biggest, blackest snake I've ever seen.

"Snake!" Joel yells again, running toward it.

Jen's laughter peals through the air as I chase after my son and grab his arm before he can reach for the snake. We watch the snake slither away, his lunch delayed by this big lug of an anxious guy whose overwhelming desire to find a snake has brought us to this back-door, out-of-the-way place.

"This is unbelievable!" Jen says, barely able to get the words out for laughing. I join in and am soon laughing hysterically, tears running down my cheeks.

"It's like he conjured it up," she wheezes. "No, it's like he wanted to see that snake so bad God said, 'Okay, Joel, here's your snake! You've got the faith, baby. Enjoy!'"

Joel looks at us with a quizzical raising of eyebrows. No words are needed to decipher his expression.

What's the big deal? I told you I wanted to see a snake!

Prayer

Oh Lord, this son of mine so often takes me to the edge of what I think I can tolerate. But what is waiting on the other side—that's the mystery I wake up to every day! Help me live in the mystery of the moment, expecting miracles instead of anticipating catastrophe. Amen.

A Shepherd's Story

*And in that region there were shepherds out in the field, keeping watch
over their flock by night. And an angel of the Lord appeared to them,
and the glory of the Lord shone around them, and they were filled with
fear. And the angel said to them, "Be not afraid; for behold, I bring you
good news of a great joy which will come to all the people; for to you
is born this day in the city of David a Savior who is Christ the Lord."*
—Luke 2:8-11

It is the Saturday before the first Sunday in Advent, and the
fellowship hall has been transformed with festive tables
dressed in red, each one a showcase for a different nativity
set. A life-size manger scene, front and center, graces the stage,
and the rich smell of pancakes, maple syrup, and sausage fills
the air. It's Breakfast in Bethlehem, an Advent program our
church puts on every year for young children and their families.

Joel has been asked to be a shepherd in the nativity play.
At age eighteen, today will be his acting debut.

The lights dim and a storyteller begins telling the familiar
tale. Mary and Joseph and a cardboard donkey slowly make
their way to the front of the room. As the story unfolds, they
knock at a door next to the stage. No one answers. They
knock again. No answer. The third time proves to be a charm.
An innkeeper greets the couple and then slowly shakes his
head back and forth. No room in the inn. He points to the
stable, giving them a lantern to light their way.

Mary and Joseph arrange themselves in a tableau in front
of an empty manger. Where's the baby? I wonder, just as a door
behind the stable opens and a girl runs out with a swaddled

doll, which she hastily hands off to Mary like a football. The audience giggles, only to be hushed by the solemn announcement of shepherds abiding in the fields behind us.

I turn to see my son dressed in full shepherd gear, headpiece and all, looking properly serious and even a little bit afraid as an angel appears and announces good news for all humankind. Holding a large stuffed lamb in his arms, Joel looks like a shepherd who would take good care of his sheep. He and his dad and three other shepherds weave their way through the assembled audience to the stable, where three of them fall to their knees. Joel and Wally stand off to the side behind Mary and Joseph. I shift my chair to get a better view.

I have eyes only for him—my son—this one labeled autistic and intellectually challenged. And Joel? Joel has eyes only for the baby Jesus. His face shines with wonder and his body speaks yearning as he stretches forward to see this gift the angel has foretold. As we sing "Silent Night," his right hand rises in worship, pointing heavenward, and then slowly lowers to point to the babe in the manger. He looks out at the audience for the first time, his entire body a question mark.

"Look! Do you see what I see?"

Prayer

Lord, today Joel heard the Good News with brand-new ears and saw Jesus born with his very own eyes. I watched him yearn with all his heart and soul and mind to point the audience toward a savior in a manger. And I thought I was coming to a children's play! O Lord, I praise you for the gift of sons—your Son and mine. Amen.

The Prayer Quilt

*I will greatly rejoice in the L\ord, my soul shall exult in
my God; for he has clothed me with the garments of
salvation, he has covered me with the robe of righteousness.*
—Isaiah 61:10a

When Joel arrived home from school today I wrapped a tangible
answer to prayer around his bulky, eighteen-year-old shoulders.

A prayer quilt, stitched and knotted with prayers for peace;
for physical, mental, and emotional healing; for wholeness as
only the Lord knows wholeness.

"This is a prayer for you," I tell him. "Prayed by people
we don't even know! They've been praying for *you* while
they sewed this quilt."

"Basketballs," Joel says with a grin as he fingers the fabric.

The story of how this prayer quilt made its way to our
home began months ago with an anxiety-venting e-mail I sent
to Barb, my cousin Jeff's wife, 300 miles away in Brighton,
Michigan.

"Dear Barb, the orthopedist has recommended surgery for
Joel's spine. His kyphosis, which is a C-curve of the spine, is
getting worse, and the doctor says there will be a lot of pain and
physical disability down the road if we don't do it. The surgery
is major. It actually involves two surgeries, and for more than
a week between the two he will be in traction as they slowly
straighten the spinal cord. Several vertebrae will be fused, and

rods will be inserted down both sides of the spine. Basically, they'll take him apart and put him back together again.

"We don't know what to do. Because of his autism and intellectual disability, we're not sure he can handle this emotionally, much less physically. How do we even begin to explain to him, in a way he can understand, what will be done?"

It wasn't long before I received Barb's reply.

"There's a quilting group at my church that gets together to pray as they make quilts for people in crisis. I've told them about Joel. We'd love to make him a quilt. Even if you elect not to do the surgery, we will pray for emotional and mental healing."

Wow.

I hit the reply button immediately. "We'd be honored."

The small package that arrived today was wrapped in brown paper and crisscrossed with masking tape. It took some tugging to remove the quilt from the box where it had been stuffed like sausage in a casing. Finally, out it popped, unfolding in waves of royal blue and sunset orange.

The quilt is sewn in a kaleidoscope of triangles of orange and blue, interspersed with patches of bright orange basketballs on a black background. In contrast, the backing of the quilt consists of a beautiful material resembling the sky on those days when the weather rapidly alternates between bright sunshine and racing clouds of gray.

Pinned to the back is a tag that reads:

Each knot on this quilt represents a prayer that was said especially for you. We hope this quilt comforts you, both spiritually and physically. The pattern of the Kaleidoscope is made entirely of triangles, symbolizing the Holy Trinity. The light and dark colors represent the light and dark periods of our life that form the overall design when seen as a whole. Brighton First United Methodist Prayers & Squares, the Prayer Quilt Ministry.

Further investigation into the box brings forth a sheet of poster-paper folded in half. The front of the card reads, "I tied a knot in prayer for you today." Inside are the signatures of more than one hundred people my family had never met.

And now, as I tuck Joel into bed, I cover him with a prayer that is as real and soft and warm as the arms of the Lord. Joel's hands rest on top of the quilt, and his beautiful smile beams up at me from the pillow.

I stand and gaze at him, transfixed.

How did the men and women of this faraway church know that the prayer I have uttered most often for my son is this: *Lord, wrap your loving arms around Joel. Make your presence as real and palpable as a warm and comforting shawl draped around his shoulders. Still his agitation Lord, and bring him peace with your presence.*

How often do we see our prayers answered in orange and blue? In knotted triangles and bright orange basketballs? How often do we tuck our prayers around our children's bodies?

I bend down to kiss Joel goodnight and then linger a few minutes longer, contemplating the visual image of a prayer spoken so many times over the years. A prayer stitched together and knotted with tears and laughter and prayers of friends in Christ we've never even met.

Prayer

Lord, thank you for this gift from the Prayer Quilt Ministry of Brighton First United Methodist Church. I never dreamed I would see my prayers answered in such a tangible, touchable, visible fashion. Still my son's agitation, Lord, and bring him peace with your presence. Amen.

An Angel Named Mohamed

And whatever you ask in prayer, you will receive, if you have faith.
—Matthew 21:22

Mohamed slips into the pew midway through the service at our church. Joel grins and grabs his hand. As they lace their fingers together, I am struck by the beautiful contrast of skin tones. Joel's complexion is peaches and cream, while Mohamed's is the color of burnished mahogany.

My mind races back to the time of turmoil five years ago, when a simple but frantic prayer was constantly on my lips.

Help, God!

While raising three boys I prayed this prayer often. When Joel hit his teens, these words passed my lips five, ten, twenty times a day. Autism was hard enough. Did we have to deal with manic swings, sleepless nights, panic attacks, and aggression, too?

Help God!

Our entire church joined us in prayer—the Tuesday-night prayer group, the e-mail prayer chain, the pastor, and the various small groups we were involved in.

As the saying goes, God moves in mysterious ways. In other words, what you ask for may come to the door in a package you never expected.

Because of the extent of Joel's disability, he was eligible for "supported living" through our county's Board of Mental Retardation and Developmental Disabilities while still living at home. We worked with a county-approved agency to find staff to support Joel with daily living activities—recreation, meals, bathing, and getting ready for bed. My husband, Wally, and I desperately needed a break after so many years of intensive care-giving.

And so the interview process began. Of the people we interviewed, good matches were at best 1 in 10. I can't even count the number of people who came through our home. They were too old to keep up with Joel's need to be on the move every minute, or too out of shape to chase him when he bolted. Too hyper. Too timid. Too loud. Too immature.

Finally, when Joel was eighteen, the agency sent a man named Mohamed. A handsome man from Mauritania, Africa, Mohamed had a firm handshake and a mantle of peace resting on his broad shoulders. Joel trusted him immediately and pulled out one of his many photo albums. They sat together on the couch, paging through the book. Mohamed smiled and pointed to one picture after another.

"Who's that? There you are with your dad at the zoo. Is that your dog? What's your dog's name?"

Yes, I thought. Finally, a match we could all live with.

"He might be on African time," my husband warned. One of Wally's good friends is from Ghana, and he had taught Wally that Western time—time lived according to the clock—is not always the most important time. Like most people with autism, Joel falls apart when his day doesn't unroll smoothly and predictably. We needed a staff person who could be counted on to be there when Joel got off the bus each day.

I explained to Mohamed the importance of being on time for Joel's comfort, not just for the sake of the clock. He understood completely and always arrived a few minutes before Joel's bus pulled up to the house.

It turned out that African time was the perfect time for Joel. Mohamed comes from a culture where life unfolds at a much less hectic pace. Unlike Americans, Mauritanians tend not to suffer from "hurry disease." With Mohamed, there's time to sit on the village green, sipping a diet cola, time to people-watch at the mall, time to hang out at the park feeding the horses or throwing bread to the fish in the pond. Over time, in Mohamed's company, Joel's anxiety slowly began to ebb.

"Do you go to church?" I asked Mohamed one day. It had been years since Wally and I had sat through an entire worship service as a couple, and it had recently occurred to us that we could possibly ask for support at church.

"I'm a Muslim," Mohamed answered. "I attend the local mosque."

"Oh . . ."

I gulped before asking the question.

"We need help with Joel in church on Sunday mornings. Would that be a problem for you?"

"That would be fine," he smiled. "We both worship the God of Abraham. I can worship in your sanctuary as well as in my mosque."

And so began a relationship that has lasted five years.

We've come to see Mohamed as a member of our family. And lonely as he is for his family in Mauritania, Mohamed has come to see us as family as well.

"I like my Mohamed. He's my brubber," Joel says at least once a day, pointing to a picture of the two of them that hangs on the refrigerator door. And when Mohamed hears from his family in Mauritania, they often ask how his "little brother Joel" is doing.

Each year we give Mohamed a gift card on his birthday—sometimes for a restaurant dinner with his friends, sometimes for clothing or sporting equipment. This year we decided to throw him a party with cake and candles. A good part of the extended family gathered to celebrate—Grandma, Uncle Dan, Aunt Julie, cousins Sam, Michael, and Stephen.

Mohamed grinned as we sang "Happy Birthday." After blowing out the candles, he said something so softly that we had to lean forward to hear.

"This is my first birthday party. Thank you so much."

I bring my mind back to the worship service. I watch Joel and Mohamed, so comfortable with one another. I am suddenly overcome by the beautiful and mysterious ways of this God we worship.

Prayer

Lord, your Word says that you are able to do far more abundantly than all that we ask or think. Never in a million years did I imagine you would answer my cry for help with a Muslim from Africa. I praise you for your gift of answered prayer, and for being a God who loves surprises as much as I do. Amen.

Kiss the Bride

And as the bridegroom rejoices over the bride, so shall your God rejoice over you.
—Isaiah 62:5b

I sit across from Joel's psychiatrist, a woman we've been working with for nearly four years, carefully choosing my words.

"Joel's brother Justin is getting married in Florida next month. The timing couldn't be worse. You know Joel's last manic cycle just about killed us. We can't chance a repeat of that for the wedding. We want to enjoy Justin's wedding, not spend the weekend dealing with sleepless nights, panic attacks, and aggression."

Joel's psychiatrist sits facing me, her legs crossed, a frown creasing her brow.

"In that case, I'd suggest you leave Joel at home, Mrs. Bolduc."

My temper flares and the words burst out before I have a chance to edit them.

"Over my dead body! This is a family event, and Joel is an important part of our family. Please write a prescription for Valium or Xanax to help him relax so *all* of us can enjoy this wedding."

We had been playing the med game for years. When Joel was eleven, before he was diagnosed with autism, our pediatrician prescribed Ritalin for his short attention span and hyperactivity. What we didn't realize at the time was that anxiety, not

A.D.D., was the underlying problem. The Ritalin exacerbated the anxiety, and obsessive-compulsive behavior surfaced with a vengeance.

Every leaf needed to be picked up off the floor. Every door needed to be closed. Every magazine put away. If something was out of place and Joel had no control over it (try getting rid of every leaf under a 100-year-old oak tree in October, or every shell off the beach next time you go to the shore), he fell apart. Nothing, short of putting everything back into complete order or leaving the scene of the crime, calmed him.

And so it began, this med game. One prescription after another was written, filled, and ingested. We quickly discovered that while someone else of Joel's age and weight needed 500 milligrams of a certain drug, Joel could only tolerate 50 or 100 milligrams. It also turned out that many medications that usually helped with autistic symptoms of agitation and aggression made Joel's symptoms worse. Each new med trial had to be taken slowly, starting at a miniscule dose until a therapeutic dose was achieved. We couldn't take him off a drug too soon, even if his symptoms worsened. It was frustrating and downright scary at times.

"Patience," the doctor repeatedly cautioned. "This takes time. We'll get it right, but it doesn't happen overnight."

Seven years later, as Joel hit eighteen, we still hadn't found the magic "cocktail" of meds that so many other parents had found for their children who were suffering from anxiety, bipolar disorder, or bouts of aggression.

I pull myself back into the psychiatrist's consulting room. "I'm serious," I continue, leaning forward. The doctor looks at me—Joel's usually agreeable and amenable mom—as if I've grown a second head.

"This wedding is the most exciting thing to happen in this family in years. We're desperately in need of making some good memories. Justin deserves a beautiful wedding." I raise my voice to make sure she understands. "That means the entire family will be present. Including Joel."

Always one to listen, the doctor pulls out a prescription pad and writes a prescription for Klonopin, an anti-seizure drug she says has been found to be effective against anxiety. It proves to be exactly what Joel needs.

Two weeks later, the morning of May 17th dawns sunny with warm, fluffy white clouds hanging suspended in the sky. After a good night's sleep, Joel wakes up with a grin.

"You gonna kiss the bride?" Joel's friend Sarah asks as he comes down for breakfast. Sarah, who has been an important part of Joel's life since he was five, has come along to help out, freeing me and Wally to play Mother and Father of the Groom.

"Elizabeth's my sister," Joel answers. "Kiss the bride."

I help him put on his brand new clothes—a dark green Hawaiian shirt and brown linen trousers to match the informal style of the outdoor wedding. His new haircut, for which he sat for the first time without squirming like a cat in a bath, makes him look five years older. He is a handsome young man.

We drive from our beach condo into the sleepy fishing village of Apalachicola and pull up to the bay-side park where the wedding gazebo, surrounded by live oak trees dripping with moss, has been decorated with white ribbons.

We hug Elizabeth's mom and dad before sitting in the front row of folding chairs. Our oldest son, Matt, joins us. My mother and sister, Julie, sit behind us, along with Wally's sister, Anne, and her husband, Ralph. A balmy breeze blows up from the bay, and the sound of birds carries on the air along with the sweet smell of magnolia. Tall, blonde, and movie-star handsome, Justin stands in front of us, awaiting his bride. Wally grabs my hand and I hold on tight.

The guitarist changes tempo and tune, and we stand and turn to watch Elizabeth, impossibly elegant, walk up the worn brick path on her father's arm, her white dress illuminated against a bluer-than-blue sky.

To my left, I hear Joel softly say, "Elizabeth's my sister. Kiss the bride." I reach out with my free arm, wrap it around his shoulder, and give him a squeeze before walking to the front of this intimate gathering of family and close friends to lead a prayer of thanksgiving for Justin and Elizabeth, and our many, many blessings.

Prayer

Dear Lord, thank you for the perfection of this day—a day that will forever live in my memory as a day of sunshine and soft ocean breezes, of family and friends, of what life is like in all its completeness. I especially thank you for our son Justin, and for the gift of his new wife, Elizabeth, the daughter I've always longed for. Bless their marriage richly, Lord. Amen.

Answered Prayer

He who dwells in the shelter of the Most High, who
abides in the shadow of the Almighty, will say to the LORD,
"My refuge and my fortress; my God, in whom I trust."
—Psalm 93:1-2

Two days before Joel's scheduled spine surgery, the
phone rings.

"Mrs. Bolduc? This is Tanya, Dr. Cook's nurse. I know
this is going to come as a surprise, but Dr. Cook has decided
to postpone Joel's surgery."

"Again? What's the reason this time?" My heart thumps
erratically.

"It's not the doctor's schedule this time, Mrs. Bolduc. He
thinks Joel's excess weight could lead to complications after
the surgery. He would like to see Joel lose fifty pounds before
operating."

I hang up the phone not knowing whether to laugh or cry.
It has taken us nearly a year to make the decision to intervene
surgically to correct Joel's kyphosis. A year of researching,
struggling, and praying.

Dr. Cook, one of the top surgeons in the country, has
assured us there is no other option. Our biggest concern
is what kind of impact this surgery will have on Joel's
emotional health. Joel will be put into a medically induced
coma for nearly a week between two separate surgeries.

Recovery will take nearly six months, several of which will entail wearing a body cast.

Joel does not tolerate Band-Aids. He rips them off and throws them across the room. He does not tolerate mosquito bites. He itches until they're a bleeding mess. Joel does not tolerate being still. He can't sit for more than five minutes. This surgery would be difficult for the world's most disciplined, cognitively aware, emotionally healthy adult. How will it impact our son?

We've asked everyone we know to pray for wisdom for both Wally and me, as well as for the surgeon. We've gone online to find other parents whose children have undergone similar procedures. The feedback has not been positive. One mother wrote back that her son complained more often of back pain *after* the surgery than before. Another mother wrote back to say that her son had died the day after the operation.

I went to bed every night wondering how I could live with myself if I chose a medical intervention for my son that caused more pain or, worse, his death.

We asked for more prayers for wisdom and discernment.

God does not always give a clear answer. We finally decided it was better to go through with the surgery now, while Joel was young, rather than wait until later. But an unexpected phone call has changed everything. There will be no surgery. At least not in the immediate future. How long will it take Joel to lose 40-50 pounds? *Can* he lose 40-50 pounds? The extra weight came on with his current medication, the only med we've found so far that helps with anxiety and aggression.

The surgery's cancellation leaves us with open calendars for the next week, so we decide to take a trip to a nearby state park. We usually rent a cabin with two bedrooms, but because we're doing this last-minute we're lucky to find a room in the lodge with two queen-size beds. After dinner and a dip in the pool, I tuck Joel into bed. When Wally returns from a walk we turn on the television. Unsaid words hang in the air between us, creating tension. An hour later we turn out the light, and I'm glad when Wally turns on his side. He's asleep and snoring within minutes. As usual, I toss and turn, my mind churning.

Suddenly I notice that Wally isn't the only one snoring. Joel is gasping and grunting, sometimes holding his breath for long intervals. I find myself holding my own, waiting to hear him breathe. Twice I climb out of bed to turn him on his side, which seems to help.

After our vacation we go in to see Dr. Cook for a follow-up appointment. I tell him about Joel's snoring.

"Sounds like apnea," he says. "If it's as bad as it sounds, it's a good thing we didn't go through with the surgery. To tell you the truth, it was more than Joel's weight that was bothering me. I awoke one night feeling like we just shouldn't follow through with it. Maybe this is the reason."

We schedule an overnight in the sleep lab. What promises to be an extremely stressful situation—pasting electrodes all over Joel's head and hooking him up to a computer—is made easier with an angel of a nurse who has a son of her own with developmental disabilities.

"You can do this, Joel," she tells him. Somehow we make it through the hook-up without using restraints. When it comes time to lie down in bed, however, the situation quickly deteriorates. Joel starts pulling wires off with both hands. It takes longer the second time to reapply them, with Wally holding his left hand and me holding his right. This time, the nurse says restraints will be necessary, at least until he goes to sleep.

Joel quickly figures out he cannot remove the electrodes, relaxes, and lets us read him a story and sing to him.

The nurse lets me into the computer room once Joel is sound asleep. The results are straightforward. Joel's airways are compromised. He is struggling to get enough oxygen through his system.

In our consultation with the pulmonary doctor, we learn that undergoing surgery with undiagnosed apnea would have been very dangerous.

All of those prayers lifted up over the past year come flooding back. Prayers for discernment and wisdom regarding the surgery. Prayers for the doctor's wisdom and discernment. Prayers for God's hand of protection.

Prayers answered, every one.

Prayer

Lord, your Word tells me that you are our fortress, that we will find refuge under your wings, that your faithfulness is a shield to those who call upon you. Thank you for giving your angels charge over my son, for guarding him by whispering to a surgeon in the middle of the night. I praise you, Lord. Amen.

Hope That Does Not Disappoint

More than that, we rejoice in our sufferings, knowing that suffering produces endurance, and endurance produces character, and character produces hope, and hope does not disappoint us, because God's love has been poured into our hearts through the Holy Spirit which has been given to us.
—*Romans 5:3-5*

We're in the car, Wally, Joel, and I, hurtling down I-75 at 65 mph, headed to a healing prayer mission led by our friends Annette and Ed Eckart. Ed and Annette are founders of Bridge for Peace, an international healing ministry.

Annette called me a few weeks ago. "How about bringing Joel to our healing mission in North Carolina next month?" As usual, the sound of Annette's exuberant voice raised my spirits. At age nineteen, Joel was still not improving in his behavior at school, and I was fighting discouragement.

I had met Annette seven years ago at a writing conference. Within hours we had made a deep, spiritual connection. When our husbands met years later, there was no doubt the four of us had been drawn together for a purpose.

I can't help but wonder if this is the reason, right now, as we speed down the highway toward this healing mission.

"The blind see, the lame walk, the deaf hear, and the Good News is proclaimed." Ed's words, spoken over the phone after their last mission to Australia, run through my mind.

Oh Lord, I believe. Help my unbelief.

As Joel listens to music on his headset, and Wally, lost in his own thoughts, drives the car, I meditate on what we've learned about healing prayer over the past several years. Jesus came to set the prisoners free, to bring sight to the blind, to release the oppressed, and to proclaim the Lord's favor.

Jesus' healings were not "proof" of his power, but an integral part of his message of freedom. He gave his followers authority to heal as he healed, along with the power of the Holy Spirit. From Annette's testimonies I know that healing can happen instantaneously. Our experience with Joel tells me that it also happens slowly, over time.

I twist in my seat and look over my shoulder at Joel. He turns from his window-watching and holds out his hand. I grab it, giving it a squeeze. I pull my hand back and blow him a kiss. He blows a kiss back. I am witnessing one result of years of soaking prayer. Traveling with Joel used to be a nightmare of whining and crying and tantrums. Today he is perfectly content to listen to music and watch the scenery fly by.

Joel has been soaked in prayer since his difficult birth. My prayers. His father's prayers. Prayers of family and friends. Prayers of the church. For years Joel loved going to the Tuesday night prayer meetings at church. The music and motion of women twirling colorful prayer flags connected with his spirit. He even enjoyed being anointed with oil and having hands laid on him during prayer, although he looked at this prayer time as something he was *doing,* not something he was *receiving.* "Let's go pray for the ladies," he often said on Tuesday mornings when he jumped out of bed.

Not long ago our small group studied healing prayer. We laid hands on one another as we prayed with the authority and power given us by Jesus. We began to see results. One of our members not only survived a massive heart attack while on a cross-country flight, but he fully recovered. Another member was healed of chronic fatigue. Still another was lifted out of depression.

Wally and I called members of the group when we were overwhelmed by living with disability. Sometimes we asked for prayer for Joel. Sometimes we asked for prayer for ourselves.

We see the results of these prayers in many ways. A deeper bond in our marriage. Joel's newfound love of Cincinnati Reds games, once impossible because of his inability to be in large crowds or to tolerate loud noises. Better eye contact. More appropriate speech. And yet Joel's healing is not complete. Still, the anxiety. Still, the aggression.

Oh Lord, I believe. Help my unbelief.

We finally arrive at the healing mission, tired but expectant. Ed and Annette welcome us with hugs and introduce us to the people gathered. A three-piece band tunes up, and we begin to worship. The weekend moves in a blur of images. Joel's hands raised in worship. The sound of many tongues in prayer. A wide-eyed Joel, taking everything in. The anointing power of the Holy Spirit, falling on the room. Hands laid on Joel, and the words, *In the name of Jesus, we command all chemicals in Joel's brain to come into divine alignment.* We're amazed as Joel comes up with a nickname, Eagle, for a young man from India with a name that's too difficult to pronounce.

We leave for home the next day. As we drive, Joel begins singing the chorus of an old Steve Miller song. "I'm going to fly like an eagle to the sea, fly like an eagle, let my spirit carry me."

Wally and I look across the front seat at one another and burst into laughter.

Prayer

Lord, thank you for the faithfulness of the friends who have soaked Joel in prayer these many years. I especially thank you for the way Joel has led us, again and again, into your presence. Lord, I believe. Help my unbelief. Amen.

The Master Weaver

This is the Lord's doing; it is marvelous in our eyes.
—Psalm 118:23

Not long after the healing mission in North Carolina, I receive a letter from my friend, Patty. I rip open the envelope to find a folded magazine article, decorated with an orange Post-it note with a hastily scrawled message: "Have you heard of the DAN program? This is an amazing story!"

I smooth the creases from the glossy magazine pages and begin to read a mother's story of her daughter's "cure" from autism, thanks to a new diet and supplement protocol called DAN, Defeat Autism Now.

I finish reading the article and sigh deeply. How many times have I dreamed of Joel talking and laughing and joking around, no signs of disability whatsoever? Could this mother's story possibly be true?

I slowly refold the article, and turn on my computer. My mind is spinning. *Am I crazy to even think about looking into this? Joel is twenty, for heaven's sake. The daughter in the article is a preschooler. All of the children the author cites as "cured" from autism are under the age of six.*

Another voice makes itself heard. *What do you have to lose? Maybe this is the answer to the prayer said over Joel in North Carolina. Remember? In the name of Jesus, we command all chemicals in Joel's brain to come into divine alignment.* If I've understood the article correctly, that's what the DAN program is all about. Healing brain chemicals by healing the gut, or digestive system, which has been damaged, reputedly, by vaccinations, prolonged use of antibiotics, or some unknown environmental factor.

Thanks to the amazing powers of Google, several hours later I have "met" two parents online, "chatted" about the program and how well their children have responded to it, found a DAN doctor in Cincinnati, and made an appointment.

I've learned that when damage in the gut is reversed through a change in diet along with the addition of supplements, major healing takes place in the brain. Behaviors in children on the autism spectrum improve greatly on this protocol. Some truly have been labeled "cured."

There is a long waiting list to get in to see the DAN physician. Three months pass before we are embarked on the program. During the three-month wait, I worry about the changes to come. No dairy? No problem. We'd already made that change, years before. No sugar or processed carbs? This will be trickier. Joel lives for his daily Icee. Slurping an Icee seems to calm him, most likely because of the deep sucking required to get the iced drink through the straw.

Other than Icees, Joel eats very little sugar. For years I thought I was being a good mom by buying crackers and pretzels instead of sugared treats. Little did I know I have been feeding Joel's addiction to carbohydrates.

It turns out that Joel's main gut problem is an overgrowth of yeast. Carbohydrates, being simple sugars, feed the yeast.

The more carbs Joel consumes, the more the yeast proliferates, and the more carbs his body craves. It's a vicious cycle.

As usual, worry turns out to be a waste of time. Changing Joel's diet is much easier than I anticipate. Again, I think of the prayer in North Carolina—*In the name of Jesus, we command all chemicals in Joel's brain to come into divine alignment.*

The Icee is replaced, temporarily, with a diet cola containing Splenda® rather than the aspartame that the DAN program forbids. Gradually, we replace the diet cola with bottled water. I clean out the pantry, throwing away crackers and pretzels and other highly processed foods. Unlike many people with autism, Joel has never been a picky eater, which makes my job easier. I buy tons of fruits, vegetables, and whole grains, and search out recipes for soups and salads. Thanks to Joel, all of us eat a healthier diet.

Within a month the healing begins. Improved attention span. Ability to follow two- and three-step directions. Lowered anxiety. Less aggression. And, miracle of miracles, his next expected manic swing does not happen. It doesn't come the next month, either. Or the next. Or the next.

I look back to that article sent in the mail with Patty's familiar handwriting on the orange Post-it note. "Have you heard of the DAN program? This is an amazing story!"

Amazing, indeed.

Is Joel "cured"? No, he is not. He still has an IQ in the "moderate" range of intellectual disability. He still struggles with behavior on an occasional basis. He is still considered to be on the autism spectrum.

Is Joel "healed"? Without a doubt. The crippling anxiety that has plagued my son for so long is gone. I remember the prayer I've spoken over him so many times—*Lord wrap your loving arms around Joel. Make your presence as real and palpable as a warm and comforting shawl draped around his shoulders. Still his agitation, Lord, and bring him peace with your presence.*

Prayer

Lord, you are so good. Your steadfast love endures forever. Your promises are sure and true. Thank you for the ways you weave our lives together, light and darkness, faith and doubt, friends and strangers and doctors. Thank you for the unending research to find a cure for autism, for the friend who sent me this article, for the courage to pursue this program, and for the healing it has brought about in Joel's neurological system. I praise your holy name. Amen.

Friends for Life

This is my commandment, that you love one another as I have loved you.
—John 15:12

Today is Joel's twenty-first birthday, and my baby's bath-room-mirror-musings—*Joel's a man; Joel's really a man; Joel's a big man*—have come to pass, legally and literally. He has chosen a bowling party to celebrate, and we fill four lanes, six people to a lane. Aunt Bin has prepared a beautiful cake, "Happy 21st Birthday" emblazoned across the top.

Three of Joel's closest friends are here—Sarah, Liz, and Stacey. They couldn't be more different personality-wise, these three young women, each of whom has played a major role in Joel's life. They're different in looks, as well. No one would ever mistake them for sisters.

Sarah is like a Norse goddess with her big bones, straight blonde hair, and sparkling blue eyes. An extrovert who loves to talk, she has been entertaining Joel with stories for years.

Liz is a couple inches short of the five foot mark, has black curly hair, and a gregarious personality. She often pulls up in front of our house, honking the horn and then jumping out of the car to holler, "Joel, I'm here!"

Stacey is tall and thin, her brown hair wavy. An introvert with a contagious belly laugh, her hazel eyes crinkle when she smiles. I'd forgotten how her smile eats up half of her face. I can't help but grin in return.

Amid the crashing of bowling pins, rock-n-roll music, and the din of several hundred people having fun, I watch these three women interact with Joel and the rest of the family. They have *become* family, these young women. They've been the daughters I never had, and I've been, I hope, a mentor to them.

Sarah entered our lives when Joel was five and she was eleven. An only child, she walked several blocks from her home to volunteer at the summer camp Joel attended. It was love at first sight. Joel was the little brother Sarah had always wanted. With his blonde hair and blue eyes, he even looked like her. Sarah "adopted" Joel, working as his one-on-one helper, which was fine with the camp counselor since Joel was a wanderer and needed constant supervision.

I loved picking Joel up from camp that summer:

"Joel had a great day, Mrs. Bolduc. He loves the water! I couldn't get him out of the pool!"

"I love this kid! He is so funny! He made up a joke today—chicken on the head! He thought it was hilarious! He makes me laugh."

"Any time you need help with Joel at home, Mrs. Bolduc, I'd be glad to come over."

And so it began, this friendship. Sarah, who lived with her single mom and found a family in us. Our boy-heavy family gained a girl.

I watch Joel open the birthday card she has brought for him today. It contains a coupon: "Good for one camping trip this summer." Sarah's always known what makes Joel happy.

She keeps him moving, signing him up for walk-a-thons. She picks him up with a car full of friends and takes him bowling. She keeps him for the night. She goes on vacation with us to the beach or the mountains, giving Wally and me some much-needed time to ourselves. Best of all, she loves and accepts Joel for who he is. *I love this kid!* Sixteen years later, her enthusiastic eleven-year-old words still echo in my memory.

When Joel gets to Liz's gift, I stifle a giggle. She called me yesterday, excited that she had found a Mr. Rogers T-shirt and keychain online. Joel used to love Mr. Rogers, and the two of them spent many an hour listening to "It's a Beautiful Day in the Neighborhood." Joel pulls the T-shirt out of the gift bag and grins at the sight of Mr. Rogers in cardigan and sneakers. He stands up and hands it to Liz. "Put it on." She helps him pull it over his head and adjusts it. I snap a picture of the two of them as Liz stands on tiptoe to give him a big hug. Joel towers over Liz these days.

Liz, like Sarah, met Joel through summer camp, where she was a counselor the year he was eight. She fell in love with his elfish grin and his high energy, which matched her own. I believe Liz is the only adult I know who can outlast Joel. She too offered to spend time with Joel after that summer at camp. Movies and swimming became their favorite outings. Returning home, Liz always filled me in on all the funny things Joel had done and said that day. "You have a really cool kid," she said one day as she dropped him off.

"Yeah, I do, don't I?" I replied. "Thanks for the reminder!"

Joel opens Stacey's present next. It's a photo album, waiting to be filled. Stacey knows that looking at pictures of the people he loves is a calming activity for Joel. We haven't seen Stacey in nearly a year. Since graduating from college with her degree in music therapy, she went back to grad school for a master's in psychology and is now working fulltime for Head Start. We've missed her. Joel still laughs whenever he picks up the ukulele and starts singing their famous theme song, "Joel Likes to Do the Trash."

What wonderful gifts God has given Joel in these three women. What unexpected gifts of grace they've been to me. I'm not in the mood to bowl today. I have too much catching up to do with the people I love.

Happy birthday, Joel. Yes, you *are* a man. A very good man, just like your dad and your brothers.

Prayer

I praise you, Lord, for Joel on his twenty-first birthday. Thank you for the blessing he has been to us over the years. And thank you for the unexpected gifts along the way—for Sarah, Liz, and Stacey—friends who love and accept Joel unconditionally, who found the funny guy hiding beneath the anxiety and behavior, who said, "I love this kid," to a mom who desperately needed to hear those words. Amen.

The Blessing

It is more blessed to give than to receive.
—Acts 20:35b

The house reverberates with laughter and the voices of thirty of our closest friends and family. Filling the house and spilling out onto the deck, they've come to join us in celebrating Joel's graduation. At age twenty-one, Joel has completed his education. How often I thought we'd never reach this milestone!

Wally and I considered throwing a huge shindig—renting a hall, hiring a caterer and a band, inviting everyone we knew. We're keenly aware that this is one of the few rites of passage Joel will experience in his lifetime. There will be no driver's license, no college graduation, no wedding day.

But Joel is the star of this party. And this star prefers intimate over splashy, quiet over loud, familiar over unfamiliar. So we pared down the guest list, bought the fixings for a backyard cookout, and peppered the yard with signs reading *Congrats, Grad!*

Joel dresses for the party in his cap and gown, the royal blue of his school colors accenting the blue of his eyes. I call him "Handsome," which elicits a grin. He runs in and out the front door as guests arrive, gown flapping, hat tilted at a rakish angle, face flushed, and eyes gleaming. He's too geared up for hugs—the guests are lucky to get a "Hi."

Aunt Julie and Joel's cousins, Samuel and Michael, help set the food on the kitchen table—baked beans and potato salad, bright strips of red, green, and yellow peppers, a bowl of watermelon, and a plate of thick-sliced tomatoes.

Wally puts off grilling the burgers until everyone arrives. An hour after the party begins my anxiety starts rising. Our party plans include a time of public blessing. We want to let Joel know that he is loved and cherished not only by Mom and Dad, but by God and everyone who knows him.

"You'd better put the meat on the grill," I whisper in Wally's ear. "Joel is getting pretty worked up. We want to make sure he's in good shape for the blessing."

"Relax. Joel's having a blast," Wally answers. "The grill will be ready in twenty minutes."

By the time dinner is ready, Joel is too excited to eat. His hat is long gone and his graduation gown hangs unzipped and crooked. I encourage him to take it off, but he refuses. He won't let me zip it up, either. Mohamed offers to take him for a short walk in the woods behind the house while everyone eats. From my seat on the deck, I follow the path of his royal-blue robe through the trees, praying that he doesn't get too agitated. *The blessing! I don't want him to miss out on the blessing!*

Mohamed and Joel reappear just as we finish eating. As I urge everyone toward the backyard where we'll form a circle for the blessing, Joel moves from guest to guest.

"Time to go home. Goodbye!"

Mohamed leads Joel into the circle that Wally has formed at the bottom of the driveway. Almost everyone Joel loves is here. Joel stands between his father and me, dancing from foot to foot, the line between excitement and agitation blurring.

"Let's join hands," Wally says. He grabs Joel's left hand, and I take his right hand. Wally turns to Joel, blinking back tears. "Joel, we want to say a prayer for you tonight." Joel stands still for a moment and looks up at his dad, his blue eyes wide.

Wally lays his hands on Joel's head. "Dear Lord, we lift Joel to you. We thank you for his presence in our lives. We thank you for the blessing he's been to everyone gathered here this evening. We praise you for his graduation from school, and we ask for your blessing to pour forth upon him as he moves forward into his future as a man . . ."

Joel yanks both hands free and runs into the center of the circle. He pumps his arm in the air, just as he did when handed his diploma at the graduation ceremony last night. "Woo hoo!" he shouts.

I've never heard a more exuberant *amen*.

Everyone laughs. While we're still standing in a circle, Joel approaches his grandma. As he reaches toward her face I wince, not knowing if his touch will be rough or gentle. But Joel simply cups her face in his hands and looks her in the eye. The laughter dies down. Joel walks to the next person in the circle, his sister-in-law, Elizabeth. He lovingly touches her on the cheek.

Oh, to know the thoughts going through his mind! Is he counting his blessings? Remembering the times Grandma watched Mr. Bean with him, laughing so hard she cried? Thinking about all the times Elizabeth and Justin spent the night with him, taking him for long walks around the lake?

I hold my breath and watch, spellbound, as Joel moves from person to person, touching each one gently. Just as I pull a tissue out of my pocket to wipe away tears, he stops in front of Miriam, whom he just met tonight. Miriam is visiting from out of town and accompanied Joel's friend Stacey to the party. Joel stops in front of this pretty young woman and stares at her. She smiles back in encouragement. Joel turns toward his brothers, who stand on the other side of the circle. He shouts, "Joel's got a girlfriend!"

The magic spell is broken by laughter and a few more "*Woo-hoos!*" The circle breaks, each one of us touched to the core by what we've just witnessed—a blessing received become a blessing given.

Prayer

Lord, once again Joel reminds me of the upside-down nature of your kingdom. What an amazing gift he gave us tonight—a clear visual image of what these oft-quoted words of yours truly mean: The kingdom of heaven belongs to the poor in spirit. Those who mourn shall be comforted. The meek shall inherit the earth. God's strength flows through our weakness. To enter the kingdom of God we must be as little children. I am blessed. Woo-hoo!

The Baccalaureate

The way God designed our bodies is a model for understanding our lives
together as a church: every part dependent on every other part, the parts
we mention and the parts we don't, the parts we see and the parts we
don't. If one part hurts, every other part is involved in the hurt, and in the
healing. If one part flourishes, every other part enters into the exuberance.
—1 Corinthians 12:25-26, The Message

We enter the sanctuary for the baccalaureate service, my gut
dancing and churning with mixed emotions. On one hand, I
am happy for Joel to be recognized as a graduate. On the other
hand, Joel has never been fully accepted by his peers at church,
and that remains a sore spot on my heart. We slip into a pew
and watch families straggle in, filling the spaces around us.
My mother, sister, and brother arrive. Uncle Dan gives Joel a
triumphant high five.

While waiting for the service to begin, I take a minute to
probe that sore spot on my heart. I think back to Joel's early
Sunday school experiences, which he negotiated with a teen
buddy named Jeff. Then came the years of aggression and
the gift of Carol and Bob, a big-hearted couple who began
a special-needs Sunday school class for Joel and two other
boys. Youth group, youth choir, yearly mission trips—none
of those dreams ever came to fruition for Joel.

Hoping to remedy that, three years ago, Wally, Joel, and I
joined the youth on a mission trip to the Galilean Children's
Home, which cares for children and adults with severe disabilities. This seemed the perfect opportunity to encourage
Joel's peers to become more welcoming of those who are

differently abled. And maybe, just maybe, Joel would make some friends.

After a rowdy three-hour ride, the kids piled out of the van to find the residents of the Children's Home waiting for us on the front porch. Our kids stopped horsing around and stared at one young boy without legs, who was supported by crutches; several children with twisted bodies sitting in wheelchairs; a mentally challenged woman jumping up and down, clapping her hands.

Joel broke away from the group and approached one of the boys in a wheelchair. He held out his hand. "Hi. My name's Joel." Wally and I looked at each other, astounded. Joel *never* takes the initiative with introductions. His greeting was the ice breaker our group needed.

I wish I could say that the rest of the week went as well. It didn't. The youth group did a great job with the residents of the Children's Home, but they never really warmed up to Joel. Maybe it was the difference between someone they were "working with" and someone they were "living with." Maybe it was the rough way he handled the kittens that lived in the barn, the way he kept touching the girls' hair, the messy way he ate his food, or his daily meltdowns. Whatever the reason, their discomfort with Joel never flowered into acceptance. I returned from that trip even more discouraged and frustrated with my inability to facilitate friendships for my son.

The sound of the youth director clearing his throat into the microphone yanks me back to the present.

"Tonight we'll invite the graduates to come up onto the chancel one by one, along with their family and friends, where we'll lay hands on them and pray for them. How does that sound?"

A few giggles ripple through the sanctuary. I look around and see several of the kids from the mission trip to The Galilean Children's Home.

One by one the youth director calls the graduates forward. All are accompanied by several friends as well as family members. The sanctuary fills with the quiet murmur of prayer. I close my eyes. *Oh Lord, where are my son's friends?*

"Joel Bolduc, will you please come forward?" I open my eyes and stand, taking Joel by the hand. We walk to the chancel, where Joel sits in a chair. As the family gathers around I watch in surprise as all of the kids from that frustrating mission trip join us in a circle around Joel. During the prayers Joel keeps his eyes wide open. Other than craning his neck to see who surrounds him, he sits perfectly still, soaking in all of the words spoken over him.

After everyone has been prayed for, the youth director calls the graduates up front again. "I have a gift for each of you," he says, holding a stack of wrapped presents in his hands. "I found a wonderful book of devotions that I thought you might enjoy."

My muddle of emotions starts to get the better of me again. *Joel can't read!*

"But for you, Joel," he continues, "I have an awesome worship CD. I watch you every Sunday, and I have to say, I've never seen anyone worship with such abandon. You've taught me a lot, Joel, about how to be free in worship. I hope this CD gives you many happy hours with the Lord."

The prayers spoken just a moment ago, combined with the youth director's words and the smile playing across Joel's face as he holds his new CD, are balm poured on that sore spot on my heart, filling me with a deep sense of the Lord's presence.

Prayer

Oh Lord, sometimes my prayers for Joel are really prayers for me, the mom who feels as if she never gets it right. Thank you for showing Joel tonight how much he is loved and appreciated. And thank you for reassuring me that, despite my shortcomings as Joel's mom, all will be well, that all will be well, that all manner of things will be well. Amen.

Easter's Promise

Now the Lord is the Spirit, and where the Spirit of the Lord is, there is freedom. And we all, with unveiled face, beholding the glory of the Lord, are being changed into his likeness from one degree of glory to another; for this comes from the Lord who is the Spirit.
—*2 Corinthians 3:17-18*

Joel and I leave the house in a hurry. I usher him into the backseat of the van, hoping to avert what looks like a potential meltdown. It's been a busy day, and he is tired and overstimulated. Driving through the entrance to Parky's Farm, past the roadside pond, I notice six unusual ducks floating peacefully in pairs on the water. Joel is anxious to see the horses, however, so we drive around to the barn and paddock and play our silly game of waving at and talking to the horses, which makes both of us laugh.

Quite often at the end of a difficult day, Joel and I take an evening drive through Parky's Farm. I always turn off the radio, open the car windows, take deep draughts of fresh air, and look for deer, rabbits, bluebirds, cedar waxwings, and great blue herons. If we're lucky, we might see a five-point buck, or a green night heron. At the age of twenty-three, Joel still likes to "wave at the horses."

We take our time driving the loop past the barn and paddock. A big piece of the sky is visible here on this hill, and it looks as if there will be a beautiful sunset. There will be no waiting to watch it tonight, though. Joel is still agitated, talking a mile a minute in the backseat, saying the same thing over and over again. "Time to go home. Have oatmeal. Time for oatmeal. It's almost dark."

Before leaving the farm I pull off the road next to the pond, wanting to identify the ducks I noticed earlier. Joel remains in the backseat while I step out of the car and walk to the edge of the water. One of each pair of ducks is dressed in coat and tails—crisp black and white, with a head crowned in deep purple. The smaller companion of each wears a feathered dress of dull brown. A cool evening breeze ruffles my hair as I watch the ducks play. One by one they dive under the water. Five, ten, fifteen, twenty seconds go by before they pop back up like corks, shaking their feathers as they surface. When bored with diving they take running leaps over the surface of the pond, half-flying, half-walking on water. My heart rises in joy as I watch their antics while breathing in the smell of spring on the breeze.

After a minute or two, Joel has had enough. He calls to me from the car.

"It's time to go home. Time for oatmeal. It's almost dark."

I barely hear him, transfixed as I am by the ducks. I watch them play for two more minutes at most, but it feels like an eternity. A deep river of peace flows through my spirit and stays with me the rest of the night.

After putting Joel to bed I turn on the computer and Google "ducks, black and white." It only takes a few minutes to identify them as bufflehead ducks. They are in the middle of their spring migration to Canada and seek out freshwater ponds to rest and feed along their journey.

During this Holy Week leading up to Easter, I can't help but think about how Jesus brings us joy and peace in times of travel and transition; how he teaches us to play, to walk on water, to dive deep for the spiritual food that satisfies. How his death on a cross and his resurrection promise us new life—the new life that is burgeoning at this very moment at Parky's Farm, in my son as he grows into adulthood, and in me as I learn to let him go.

Prayer

Lord, so often when I come to this place with Joel I find you waiting to meet me. Tonight, watching the antics of those beautiful ducks in the pond, I felt for a moment as if I were standing in the glory of your presence. Thank you for reminding me during this Holy Week that you are in the business of redemption and transformation, that both my son and I are slowly but surely being changed into your likeness as we go about our days together. Amen.

Finding the Alleluia

*For you shall go out in joy, and be led forth in peace; the
mountains and the hills before you shall break forth into
singing, and all the trees of the field shall clap their hands.*
—Isaiah 55:12

It is 8 a.m. Only ten minutes until the bus pulls up, honks the horn, and wheezes away, taking Joel to work.

Only ten minutes until I am free to pack my bags for a much-anticipated writing retreat. The Ursulines are graciously allowing me the use of a cottage on their grounds one night a week for the next ten weeks. Dedicated writing time, away from the responsibilities of home, is a gift. My mood matches the sunny day outside the kitchen window.

I'm making Joel's lunch and ruminating on what chapter subject I'll tackle later in the day when Joel runs through the kitchen, shouting, "I have to poop!"

At age twenty-three, Joel still does not realize the world is not necessarily interested in his bathroom habits.

The next thing I know, the entire morning is falling apart.

"Oh no!" Joel yells from the bathroom.

I shove the turkey wrap I've just made into a sandwich bag before heading for the bathroom.

"What's up?" One glance tells the story. The toilet is clogged. Joel stands with his hand on the flush valve, and his face lets me know this story is not going to have a happy ending.

I keep my voice cheerful. "It's okay, Joel. Let's go find the plunger."

"No! Water!" he yells, his face scrunched in anxiety over this kink in his morning routine.

"Let's go find the plunger," I repeat, not quite as cheerfully. Joel flushes the toilet again.

This time I yell. "NO!" We watch, helpless, as the dirty water rises dangerously near the top of the toilet bowl.

I put my arm around Joel and guide him out of the bathroom, through the kitchen, and upstairs. "Plunger, buddy."

The plunger is nowhere to be found. We head back down to the kitchen. Somehow, I have to keep him out of the bathroom. Time for a little redirection.

"Help me finish making your lunch, bud. I need a bottle of water and the cold pack."

No way. Joel runs for the bathroom.

"Water gone!" he cries.

I shove various sandwich bags full of lunch goodies into the lunch box and reach for Joel's backpack.

I hear the sound of the toilet flushing again. Once. Twice. Three times. I enter the bathroom just in time to watch the dirty water flow up and over the top of the bowl and cascade all over the floor.

Joel is frantic. He reaches for the toilet handle again. I grab his arm and pull him out of the bathroom before he steps in the mess. Just then the bus pulls up and honks the horn. I gasp a sigh of relief. "Bus is here, Joel. Grab your coat."

"No bus. Fix water!" he yells, heading back for the bathroom. I grab him in a one-armed hug and guide him toward the door. I'm barefoot, still in my pajamas, with my jacket thrown on for warmth on this cool May morning.

"No bus! Stay home!" By now we're both in the front yard. Several curious faces peer out the bus windows.

"I'll fix the toilet while you're at work, Joel. I promise. Just get on the bus."

After five minutes of wrangling, I'm finally able to lead Joel to the door of the bus. He climbs on, crying. "No work! Stay home! Fix water!"

"Hey, Joel," the bus driver says cheerfully. Then he looks at me. "You better put some shoes on, Mrs. Bolduc," he laughs.

"Yeah, right," I mutter, looking down at my bare legs and feet, my new nail polish, Tahitian Sunset, sparkles dancing in the morning sun.

I drag myself back into the house, as my I-have-two-days-to-myself-to-write-read-and-pray mood soured. It takes ten minutes to clean up the mess.

An hour later, in the car, I call my friend Patty, hoping to find a way out of the cloud that has darkened my morning. I can't believe my son is twenty-three and I am still dealing with these kinds of messes. Luckily Patty is home. I tell her the tale of our poopy morning. She laughs. I laugh.

"The not-so-funny thing is I'm on my way to finish working on *Autism & Alleluias*. Where in the world is the alleluia in a poopy morning?" I ask with a groan.

I can hear the smile in Patty's voice. "You know, Kathy, I seem to remember that quite a few of your chapters begin with a groan before you get to the *alleluia*. The *alleluia* is there. You just haven't found it yet."

So, here I sit, four hours later, on the front porch of this beautiful old cottage. The house is situated on a tree-studded lawn that slopes down to a stream. As the trees dance in the wind, golden sheets of pollen drift past in waves. A bright red cardinal flits and flutters back and forth from maple to oak to linden tree.

And it occurs to me that without Joel, without autism, without this book, I never would have found this place. An *alleluia* rises in my chest. Patty was right. *Alleluias*, like births, often begin with a groan. With that realization, the weight of the morning dissipates and blows away on the breeze.

It's time to get to work.

Prayer

Dear Lord, it has been twenty-three years since my last experience of labor and birth, and I seem to have forgotten that joy always follows the pain. It's called labor for a reason—giving birth is hard work. Remind me that I give birth every day as I grow more and more into the person you created me to be. This daily act of creation is hard work, but each day, no matter how painful, holds an alleluia if I just keep my eyes open. Open the eyes of my heart, Lord. Amen.

Transitions

For I know the plans I have for you, says the LORD, plans for welfare and not for evil, to give you a future and a hope.
                                        —Jeremiah 29:11

I stand with Joel's work supervisor, Rhonda, and watch Joel unwrap a bar of soap for reprocessing. He plunks the soap into one container and throws the wrapper into another. He grabs another bar and begins again.

"He's doing great," Rhonda says. "He's working twenty, maybe thirty minutes before he gets distracted, and then he takes a break before getting back to work."

My eyes roam the room. Another young man works at a table across from Joel. A treadmill stands in one corner. United States and world maps add color to one wall. Below them sits a computer. A wave of gratitude nearly knocks me over.

The path to this place—Beckman Adult Center—has been rocky and full of heartache. A year ago Joel's team began meeting monthly to plan a smooth transition from school to work. Each of us had Joel's best interests in mind, but we had different ways of looking at the options.

"We need to find a job for Joel where movement is a part of his daily routine."

"Our top priority should be a high staff-to-client ratio. Joel needs one-on-one support."

"Joel would do better in a leisure program. He's not motivated by money."

Wally stood firm in his belief that Joel needed to work. "I work. Kathy works. Joel's brothers work. Work is what we do as adults. Work will give Joel a sense of accomplishment."

We spent weeks discussing options and visiting potential work and leisure sites where support, however minimal, was provided.

A new program was opening at Parky's Farm, one of Joel's favorite places. Students would be trained to feed animals, clean out barns, and groom horses.

"This is perfect for Joel," I told Wally after meeting with the project director. "He'll be outside with plenty of movement, and he can work with the horses!"

What we didn't anticipate was how Joel's familiarity with Parky's Farm would breed discontent with a work structure. In Joel's mind, Parky's Farm meant fun, not work. His frustration level rose and, along with it, anxiety. With the anxiety came the old behaviors. Hairpulling. Cussing. Exposing himself.

Three weeks into the program we received a phone call from the director. "I'm sorry to disappoint you, but the success of this program depends on the image we present to the public. This program is not a good fit for Joel."

Devastated, I scheduled another team meeting. Graduation was only five months away, and we were down to what we thought of as our last viable option, a program offering both work and leisure programs with some community interaction. With Joel's input we decided upon three days a week at their laundry facility, where he would learn to sort and fold

127

laundry. He would spend the other two days at their sports facility, where he would participate in games and spend time at community sports venues.

The first two months went smoothly. Joel spent time weekly at both facilities, accompanied by his one-on-one staff from school. When that support was removed, however, Joel's anxiety, and the behaviors that accompany it, escalated.

The team decided that Joel needed the consistency of one site per week instead of two. Joel chose the sports facility. After several phone calls from staff complaining that Joel was "wandering" and two days of observation on our part, we pulled Joel out of the program, feeling that there was not enough staff to monitor his movements closely.

Beckman Adult Center, our last choice because it was a re-stricted environment with no community involvement, began to look more interesting. It did have several advantages. It sat across the street from Joel's school, and the same bus com-pany provided transportation. The staff was extremely well trained and creative in dealing with behavior issues.

The day I signed Beckman's paperwork, Walter Vaughn, former vice-principal of Joel's school, called me.

"I am so excited to hear that Joel is joining us at Beckman," he said in his characteristically exuberant voice. "I will do everything in my power to make this a successful transition for Joel. I'm fixing up a room for him with just one other cli-ent and two supervisors. That way, he will have one-on-one support for a while. We'll transition him out to the floor when he's settled in.

"And I'm going get a treadmill for him to use when he's anxious, and we'll set up a picture schedule like the one he used in school. Change is hard for Joel, so we'll make things as familiar as possible for him."

Here we are, a few weeks later. Joel is hard at work, unwrapping soap. He doesn't have to sit—he can work standing up. He's free to take a break whenever he needs one. He feels safe here and comfortable, confident in himself and his ability to do his job.

Yes, work gives us shape and purpose to our days. Just like his mom, dad, and brothers, Joel now has a job that he enjoys. And, as his brother Justin told him, "Getting that paycheck feels pretty darn good."

Prayer

Dear Lord, there have been so many twists and turns on this journey, I've often wondered if we would find our way. When will I learn that you are faithful not in some things, but in all things? I'm beginning to catch a glimpse of the overall plan you've laid out for Joel. Walter was the one member of Joel's team who saw my son's deepest need—a need for familiarity in a sea of change—and did everything in his power to meet that need. Thank you, Lord, for the plans you have for Joel. Thank you for your faithfulness. And thank you for Walter. Amen.

Swimming with the Honu

Deep calls to deep at the thunder of the cataracts; all thy waves and thy billows have gone over me. By day the LORD commands his steadfast love, and at night his song is with me, a prayer to the God of my life.
—Psalm 42:7-8

"One last swim before we go home?"

Wally stands knee deep in the sea-green waters of Kalihiwai Bay on the northern shore of Kauai. It's the last morning of our thirty-fifth anniversary trip to Hawaii, and we have less than two hours before heading to the airport.

"No," I answer. "We still have to pack, and I don't want to wash my hair again."

I wade into the water and let the gentle surf break over my ankles. I'm mesmerized by the lapping waves, the fragrant breeze, and the myriad shades of blue and green spread out in a visual feast before me.

I scan the clear water around me for honu, the giant sea turtles that frequent the waters of this bay. We've spent hours over the past twelve days watching the graceful movements of these ancient sea creatures, older than the dinosaurs and now on the world's endangered species list. I want to say goodbye.

"No turtles today," I call out to Wally. He doesn't hear me. The words of the song "Don't Worry, Be Happy" run through my mind as I watch him lazily float on his back, paddling in circles.

For heaven's sake, I mutter to myself, *this is your last chance, Kathy.* Stuffing my hair into a baseball cap, I wade waist deep before sinking back into the cool water. Submerged, I relax into the undulating movement of the waves, my spirit expanding with an audible sigh of gratitude.

This vacation was a lifelong dream. While Wally and I have always made time for romance with weekend getaways and an occasional weeklong vacation, we've never felt comfortable leaving Joel for more than seven days.

I've been dreaming about Hawaii for as long as I can remember, but it was too remote for a one-week trip. Not long after Joel turned twenty-one, Wally turned to me and said, "I think it's time we started planning that vacation to Hawaii. Let's celebrate our thirty-fifth anniversary there!"

I ran to my study, turned on the computer, and started planning the trip.

Hawaii is all I had dreamed it would be. The clichés are true. It's paradise. Over the past twelve days we've spent hours exploring canyons and rainforests and deserted beaches. Rode a boat along the Nepali coastline, one of the most beautiful places on earth. Drank wine while watching spectacular sunsets. Snorkeled among schools of colorful parrotfish. Ordered carryout sushi for lunch and ate it on the beach after taking a swim.

Just yesterday Wally put his arm around me and pulled me close. "Will you forgive me for waiting so long to bring you here?" he asked with a frown.

I leaned over and kissed him. "There was a reason we didn't come earlier," I said. "But we're here now and that's all that counts. Right now. Here. Today."

I'm paddling, like Wally, in circles when a motion off to my right catches my attention. Turning my head, I see the round, green head of a honu, just ten yards away. Slowly, I swim toward her.

Within a few feet of this magnificent sea creature, I stop and tread water. She stares at me from ancient hooded eyes. Her flippers gently cut through the water. I match her rhythm and motion, swimming alongside in a steady breast stroke.

Suspended in the womb of creation, we swim slowly as if we have all the time in the world. My anxiety about packing, cleaning the condo, enduring the interminable plane ride home, and making decisions about Joel's future slough away in the salty green waters of Kalihiwai Bay.

It lasts two minutes at most, this goodbye swim with my honu friend. And yet, it lasts an eternity. We swim side by side, tethered to our Creator, and connected to one another. Connected by the rhythm of the sea. Connected by the rhythm of the life force pumping through our bodies. Connected by the measured cadences of creation itself.

Prayer

Lord, thank you for this dream-come-true, for the beauty of your creation, for this husband, for thirty-five years together. Thank you for my honu friend and for the magic of our time together. Thank you for this life I live, with all of its ups and downs and twists and turns. Help me learn to live in the moment, Lord, as Joel has so often taught me. Right here. Right now. Today. Amen.

Princess Pocahontas

So out of the ground the LORD God formed every beast of the field and every bird of the air, and brought them to the man to see what he would call them; and whatever the man called every living creature, that was its name.
—*Genesis 2:18-19*

The winter sun is just peeping through the east window of the living room as I sit in my favorite chair reading the paper over a steaming cup of tea. Joel is sitting on the floor in front of me with his black lab, Poco. We're waiting patiently for the bus to pick up Joel for work.

It's a longstanding ritual, this morning floor time. Joel lies on top of the dog and then rolls off. He sits in front of her, squeezes her snout, and looks her in the eye. Always the first to defer, she looks away. Joel pats her on the back, none-too-gently. Tail wagging, she rolls over, begging for a tummy rub. Joel rubs for a moment and then pulls on her back leg instead. Poco thrashes around like a wild woman, all four legs in the air, managing to scratch her back and shed black hair on the oriental carpet all at the same time. She's obviously loving every minute of it.

I once asked the vet if I should worry about Joel's lovingly rough treatment of his dog.

"Is her tail wagging, or is she trying to escape?" he asked.

"She just sits there and takes it, her tail wagging the whole time," I answered.

"Then don't worry. You can hardly over-touch a lab. They thrive on touch, even if it's a little on the rough side."

I dubbed her Saint Poco that day, for her patience and forbearance. And I began to notice that after just ten minutes of floor time with his dog, Joel became visibly calmer. It became a great way to start the day for the next thirteen years.

I think back to the day we brought her home, a six-week-old black bundle of energy and love. Joel was ten, and our old dog, Blue, who had grown up with Matt and Justin, had recently died. How could we ever replace Blue, we wondered? Blue was the world's best dog—a boy's dog—a dog's dog, for that matter. Everybody loved Blue. We guessed at her parentage. Maybe a mix between a sheepdog and a husky? How else to explain the ice-blue eyes (for which we named her Suite Judy Blue Eyes)? The shaggy fur? The herding instinct?

Blue lived and died before the leash law ruined the lives of all dogs to come. She made her daily neighborhood rounds, stopping at corners and looking both ways before crossing the street (cross my heart and hope to die!). She found lost children (Justin, when he "ran away" with a food-filled bandana on the end of a stick, hobo style). She played with the boys in the woods behind our house and visited lonely widows and widowers. What kind of dog could live up to that legacy?

From the very beginning, Poco was Joel's dog. Matt was away at college, and Justin was busy with school, work, and golf. When we began to think about buying another dog, we found a trainer who said he could train a dog to protect Joel—to keep him from going into the street, from wandering away from the yard, from accepting the advances of strangers. The trainer's program was expensive, but we figured it was worth the cost in order to give Joel some semblance of independence.

The trainer sent us to a woman who bred Labrador retrievers. We found Poco in the very first litter we looked at. She caught Justin's eye with all of her puppy energy and sweet disposition. He picked her up, gave her a kiss, and then held her out to Joel. When she licked Joel's hand and made him giggle, the decision was made.

We took her home and named her Princess Pocahontas, Poco for short. She quickly settled in as a member of the family. Joel walked her every day (with assistance), and floor time together became part of their morning routine.

Unfortunately, the trainer disappeared after puppy training. As we had paid him up front, our hopes for a "disability dog" disappeared along with him. Matt came home from college and worked with Poco for hours, making great strides with her. But, when he went back to school, Poco reverted to jumping on visitors and straining at the leash. No, she wasn't as smart as Blue, who had trained like a dream. No, she didn't know how to visit the neighbors and return home in an hour or two. She bolted whenever Joel opened the door and disappeared for hours (one time for days), following joggers home and making herself at home in their front yards. No, she didn't look both ways before crossing the street. One dreadful night she was struck by a car in front of our house, but luckily came through the accident with no more than bruising and hurt pride.

No, she isn't like Blue, but as I watch Joel play with her this morning, I realize how very much we will miss Poco when she goes to doggy-heaven, free to run with dogs like Blue, who didn't grow up with a leash law. I no longer care that we were "taken" by a disreputable trainer, that she never learned to keep Joel in the yard. We've all fallen in love with Princess Pocahontas. She turned out to be the best possible dog for Joel— quiet, gentle, loyal, patient, and yes, downright saintly.

Prayer

Dear Lord, you are faithful even in the little things. A boy and his dog—it's a mythic theme throughout literature. I'm so happy all three of my boys were able to experience the love of a good dog. And I'd like to know, before I get there myself—are there dogs in heaven? Amen.

Letting Go

I remember the days of old, I meditate on all that thou hast done; I muse on what thy hands have wrought.
—Psalm 143:5

The time has come. The time is now.

Words from a Dr. Seuss book reverberate through my mind as Wally and I talk about transitioning Joel into his own home with 24-hour staffing.

The time has come. The time is now. Marvin K. Mooney will you please go now!

A quote I recently used in a speech comes to mind. "Life is lived forward but understood backward." I look backward to remember how this letting go has been done before.

I see Matt, our firstborn, snuggled on my lap while I read his favorite Dr. Seuss book, *Marvin K. Mooney.* How he loved to beat me to the punch line—*Marvin K. Mooney will you please go now!*

I see Matt again in my mind's eye, twenty-four years old with an engineer's mind, calculating down to the exact inch how many boxes his Toyota truck bed would hold, as he prepared for the move from Ohio to California. Just out of graduate school, he had taken a job in Sacramento. He would not accept any help with the packing. He also made it clear that he did not need any help with the 48-hour drive. He would manage just fine on his own, thank you very much.

I remember standing in the front yard, watching my first-born son throw his backpack and coffee cup in the front seat as he prepared to leave home for a new life thousands of miles away. The look on his face when he turned to look at me was apologetic, and at the same time, tenacious.

I cleared my throat and handed him my cell phone.

"I want you to call every eight hours, and let us know where you are," I said. "Then mail the phone back to me when you get there."

He grinned sheepishly as he took the phone, his one concession to a mom who couldn't quite let go. He gave me a hug and a kiss and then hugged his brothers and dad. We took a few more pictures as he climbed into his truck, waved, and drove away.

With the second-born, there's the advantage of having done this letting-go thing before, although there is the complication of different personalities. In high school, Justin had become an avid golfer, nicknamed The Stallion by his coach for his long blonde mane of hair and independent, cocky attitude. Letting Justin go meant watching him quit college to move to Florida for a golf course job and a stab at getting his PGA card. It meant watching him leave that job to come home to support his ex-girlfriend, just diagnosed with brain cancer. It meant watching him struggle to figure out what the next step might be.

One Mother's Day he took me out for coffee.

"I'm thinking about going back to school to get a degree in construction management, so I can work for Dad," he said. "Do you think that's the right decision?"

I told him his dad's business had been a great source of income, while affording Wally plenty of time to spend with his family. I said there was no way I could tell him whether or not this was the right decision for him, but that I was confident in his ability to decide. I assured him I would pray for him and that I loved him very much.

Justin went on to earn several awards through college, graduated with a degree in construction management, married our beautiful daughter-in-law, Elizabeth, and now works with his father in the crane business.

Painful? Gratifying? The natural course of things? Yes, yes, and yes.

Today Joel is just a few months short of twenty-four. A voice in my spirit whispers, *The time has come. The time is now.* I feel it in my bones, the rightness of it. Wally and I have said from the very beginning that Joel, like his brothers, should have the opportunity to live as independent a life as possible.

The time has come. The time is now.

I think back to Joel's birth. The fetal monitor, screaming that the baby was in distress. Specialists rushing into the birthing room. Our just-born son, being rushed away to the side of the room. And then came the afterbirth. The placenta, attached with ferocity to the side of my uterus, would not let go. Having undergone the birth naturally, I thought I would die of pain as the doctor ripped the placenta from my body. He told me I was lucky to be giving birth in 1985—that I may not have survived in the early 1900s.

This letting go feels like that. Scary and painful and

potentially dangerous. *Breathe deep,* I told myself during all three of my natural birth experiences. *Relax into the contractions. You can do this. Women have been doing this since the beginning of time.*

The time has come. The time is now. This is part of the cycle of life. Joel, like his brothers, is his own person. He doesn't need a mother hovering over him on a daily basis, wiping his face and tying his shoes. There is a world out there for him to explore, people to meet, experiences to enjoy.

The time has come. The time is now.

Prayer

Dear Lord, I am counting on you to help us through this letting-go process. We can't do it without you. Looking back, I see you've been with us every step of the way. I've come to trust you, Lord. I know you won't abandon us now. Once again, I hand my son over to you. Help me to open my fingers and give him over gracefully, instead of clutching him to my breast like a suckling child. Remind me that your love for him is far greater than my own. Amen.

*The L*ORD *will fulfill his purpose for [my son];*
*thy steadfast love, O L*ORD*, endures for ever.*
                                              —*Psalm 138:8*

Also from Kathleen Deyer Bolduc

His Name is Joel: Searching for God in a Son's Disability

"Kathleen Bolduc holds her life, and her family's life, in one hand, a Bible in the other, and shares with us the sometimes clashing, sometimes confirming, often revealing process of bringing the Story into focus with her story. It reads and feels very real, very honest, very unpretentious, and thus, very holy—just as she, in fact, would say she learned to 'read' her son." —Bill Gaventa, director of Community and Congregational Supports, Elizabeth M. Boggs Center on Developmental Disabilities; editor, *Journal of Religion, Disability and Health*

"I wish everyone could read this book! It is a work of art, a timeless meditation, a wise insight, a deep sigh, a fresh breeze, a good chuckle, and a healing therapy, all rolled into one. In 127 pages of easy-to-read-in-5-minute pieces, Ms. Bolduc gives an honest, straightforward tour through the inner and outer experience of a parent whose child has a disability." —Rev. Sarah Eastes, director of Training and Public Education, Council for Retarded Citizens; author of *Agenda for Real Life*

A Place Called Acceptance: Ministry with Families of Children with Disabilities

"A powerful resource for congregations who want to be communities of welcome and encouragement for families of children with disabilities. In an amazing economy of pages, the author's own moving story of parenting a child with disabilities provides a portal into clear, concrete ways every congregation can take to experience the value of including families with special needs—and special gifts—in the life of the people of faith." —Diana R. Garland, dean, Baylor School of Social Work; author of *Family Ministry: A Comprehensive Guide*

Visit www.kathleenbolduc.com where you can:

- Order His Name is *Joel* and *A Place Called Acceptance*
- Learn more about the author
- Read Kathy's blog
- Check the author's schedule of speaking engagements
- Contact Kathy